MW00899397

THE PROBLEM IS NOT AVAILABLE

364 Days in Sudan

Anila Prineveau Goldie

ISBN: 978-1-4834-1553-6 (sc)
ISBN: 978-1-4834-1841-4 (e)

Library of Congress Control Number: 2014916711

Because of the dynamic nature of the Internet, any web addresses or links contained in this book may have changed since publication and may no longer be valid. The views expressed in this work are solely those of the author and do not necessarily reflect the views of the publisher, and the publisher hereby disclaims any responsibility for them.

Any people depicted in stock imagery provided by Thinkstock are models, and such images are being used for illustrative purposes only. Certain stock imagery © Thinkstock.

Lulu Publishing Services rev. date: 12/09/2014

DEDICATION

This book is dedicated to my grandfather, John Robert Goldie White, "Jack,"
and to my great aunt, Sara A. Prineveau, "Sadie,"
with gratitude for years of support and love.

If there be righteousness in the heart, there will be beauty in the character. If there is beauty in the character, there will be harmony in the home. If there is harmony in the home, there will be order in each nation. When there is order in each nation, there will be peace in the world.

--Anonymous

THANK YOU

It takes a village and I am deeply grateful to the many friends who collectively amassed thousands of hours of heart-felt generosity while contributing to: healing my injured foot so I could leave Seattle for Sudan, my experience in Sudan, and to the making of this book.

I want to thank Ray for believing in me through it all, Seumas who toted his flaming-red harp to my hospital room and healed my injured foot while he played traditional Scottish tunes whereupon I could go home and prepare for my two years in Khartoum (even though I did arrive a month late and had only been off crutches for one day). More thanks go to the friends who sent me flowers, cards and music, and brought tasty food for me to eat, Lynn for being with me before and after the surgeries, Deborah and Jane for bringing me groceries, Peter Pie who fetched my prescriptions and told me I had to go see those whirling dervishes, Paddy and Austin for packing all of my belongings for twelve hours a day, six days in a row while I stood on crutches and watched because I couldn't yet put any weight on my ailing foot, Jane who hosted a memorable going-away party for me, and Kennedy who told me, "You are going for all of us. None of the rest of us could do this. It takes more than most of us have. Bring your stories home and share them," Deborah and John for inviting me to stay in their house until Lorna came to take me to the airport and never mind the fact that we were having so much fun talking while we ate breakfast that we lost track of time and I missed that flight to Khartoum, the friends who sent me care packages from Seattle especially Jane who always tucked in Scottish shortbread, the friends who hosted a rockin' birthday party and gave me places to stay in their homes during my summer break in Seattle, Peter and Susan who distributed the letters I sent home, and Jerry who encouraged me to publish them.

Thank you to Mingtang for guidance and 182 Russians for support in Shaolin, China, where I understood how to organize this book and which stories to tell during a summer of deep meditation.

Thank you to Steve who set me on the correct writer's course of action, the other Lorna for encouragement and networking, Barbara for tips, Pamela for convincing me of the need for literary arc, Greg for loads of technical support, Carol for editing, Carolyn for editing, technical support, sharing my enthusiasm and a place to stay for a week when we were snowed in because we'd stayed up until 2 a.m. working on the book while an unexpectedly ferocious snow storm descended, Penny and Dale for recording this book and accepting my offer to weed their yard in exchange, Mike and Lisa for user-friendly tech support and friendship sprinkled with much laughter, Jerry for timely, intelligent, compassionate copy editing and saving me from a bad ending, the Edmonds Writers' Group for perspective, Cécile for support in keeping with the star-thrower tradition, and Oreste for executive coaching.

Many thanks to Muhammad Wardi's uplifting music on the *Live in Adidas Ababa* album which I played daily in Khartoum as well as during thousands of hours while I, a quintessential extrovert, wrote and rewrote this book in solitude while listening to Wardi and hundreds of world music, gospel, rhythm and blues, and classical musicians. Thank you for keeping my spirits on the up and up.

Thank you to Fatima, Helen, and Shane for Khartoum camaraderie, Ashraf and his family for a family of the heart in Khartoum, and countless Sudanese citizens for kindness, generosity, gentleness, and authenticity.

All of you will hold a special place in my heart and mind forever.

CONTENTS

D

E

F

G

H

I

J

K

L

M

N

O

P

Q

R

S

T

U

V

W

X

Y

Z

PREFACE

My future always calls to me long before I'm ready to answer.

When I got the job offer to teach in Khartoum, Sudan, I knew I had been called. The calling had come in a prophetic dream. These prophetic dreams are different from the others. They arrive swiftly, last only for an instant, and appear in twilight colors. I don't have these dreams often. When I do have them, I know. This time the dream was simply of a one-humped camel in a desert, and it had been coming to me for months. I had no idea what it meant until I got the offer, seemingly out of the blue, to teach in Khartoum.

Along with the dream, I had called in the offer for the job with this prayer: Thank you for bringing me the job that is in my highest good, the highest good of all the lives I will touch, and in the highest good of all those whose lives will touch me.

Eleven hours into my prayer vigil my phone rang and it was Bob, my future boss, with the job offer to teach in Khartoum. Bob had discovered I was looking for my next teaching position through a former high-school buddy with whom he, for forty years, had exchanged Christmas cards. When Bob was in Seattle for his mother's funeral, he was invited to his old friend's house for dinner where Bob saw my résumé sitting on a table. He asked about me, penciled my name and phone number on a scrap of paper, stuffed it into his wallet, forgot about it, found it three months later, and called me.

"Something tells me," he said, "you're the right person for the job. I'm returning to Khartoum in ten days and I need to have a person hired before I leave the States. I've got a couple of people on the back burner, but I think you're it."

For the next forty-five minutes we discussed details about the school, the teaching position, and life in Khartoum. He ended the conversation saying, "I want to hire you. You've got five days to make your mind up. If I haven't heard from you, I'll call you back in five days."

I knew I had met my destiny, but I couldn't quite say yes, and I couldn't figure out why I was hesitating. I'd never before hesitated to live in a foreign country. I was a successful and seasoned teacher and traveler with a bachelor's degree in cultural anthropology and a master's degree in education. I'd thrived on teaching in exotic cultures, and travelling and living in far-flung places. Journeying with a thin wallet and an open heart, I took great pleasure in interacting with local people on all continents.

When I dug deep into my psyche I realized I was afraid to live in Khartoum. After two days of asking myself, Why are you afraid? I knew I was afraid to live in a Muslim country. I pride myself in keeping an open mind and an open heart. I was astounded at the reason for my fear. The only way to meet this kind of fear is to walk into the center of it. This is what I did when I accepted the job offer to teach English literature to sixth through twelfth graders in a private school in Khartoum for two school years. This amounted to a total of 364 days.

It has been said that the deepest lessons are learned in the desert. I certainly learned my share of lessons in the rich desert of Sudan where I set out to befriend my fear of Muslims through making friends with the Muslim Sudanese. Why did I do this? Because, when one befriends a fear then that fear ceases to control you, and an opening is created for true understanding; this brings the fruits of connection and caring. I returned home having made friends with my fear.

In this alphabet of up-close and personal stories you will discover an unfolding of the Sudanese people and their culture which, in many ways, is exotic compared to ours and in other ways not very different at all. They, too, are peace-loving and they love their culture and country just as much as you and I love ours. A deep desire to share stories from this vantage point is what compelled me to write this book which is a compilation of vignettes from my letters home written from 1996 through 1998 when Sudan was rarely in the Western news and little known to Westerners. At present, as a result of ongoing news reports, Sudan is well known as a war-torn, predominately Muslim country. I experienced a Sudan where the people, despite their numerous challenges, are indefatigably warm-hearted, sensitive, protective, and generous. This is the Sudan I am passionate about sharing.

Now I invite you, the reader, to experience rare and authentic stories written from inside a country where not many Westerners are permitted to reside for an extended period of time and thus very few receive invitations into the homes, mosques, and hearts of the Sudanese as I did.

HOW TO USE THIS BOOK

The pronunciation and definition of Arabic words, phrases, and place names are in the glossary which can be found at the end of the book.

The stories are arranged in alphabetical order and can be read in chronological order, or independent of each other.

General categories with corresponding chapter numbers are listed below:

Food: 6, 35, 42, 43, 49, 53, 54
Global Family and Global Village: 3, 18, 68, 70
Men: 7, 8, 21, 22, 26, 28, 29, 45
Police State and War: 2, 13, 40, 50, 63, 65
Scottish Heritage: 4, 58, 69
Spirituality and Spirits: 1, 16, 23, 32, 33, 51, 57, 64, 66
Sudanese Attitudes: 12, 60, 61, 62
Sudanese Culture: 9, 10, 11, 17, 19, 20, 25, 27, 30, 36, 37, 41, 46
Travel: 5, 24, 34, 38, 39, 47, 48, 52, 55, 59
Women: 14, 15, 31, 44, 56, 67

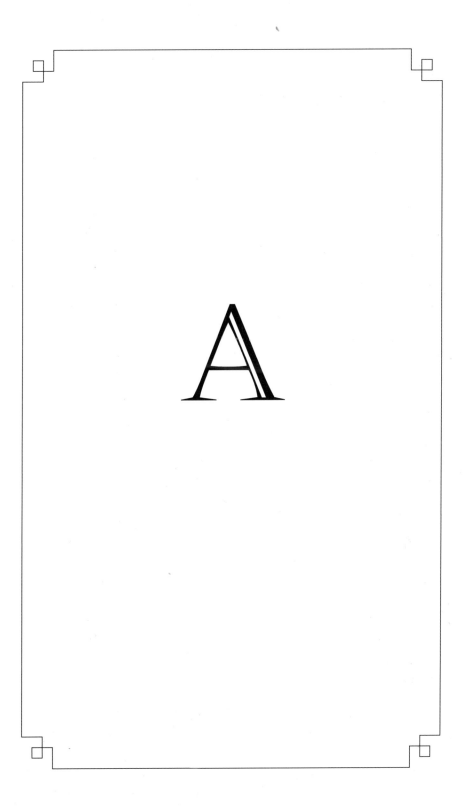

Chapter 1

ABU MEDINO

Abu Medino looked the part of the pied piper of Sudan as he cavorted with a twelve-foot long, dead, sea snake draped across his shoulders, and the shoulders of the two children whom he'd enticed to frolic with him. Their laughter caused everyone in the resort to laugh, too. While Abu was merrymaking with the dead sea serpent, Muhammad my guide and translator walked up to me, pointed to Abu and said in broken English, "Abu save you life today. You know this?"

I said an incredulous, "What? Abu saved my life? How? I haven't seen Abu since I said goodbye to him late last night."

Muhammad then explained to me that this snake carries deadly venom and it is aggressive. Earlier in the day the snake was stalking me while I was snorkeling, and Abu killed the snake before it killed me.

I was stunned. My mind raced with irrational disbelief for several seconds. What? He saved me? What? I'm in great shape. I swam competitively for years. I know myself in the water. I love the water and, and, oh, oh, I get it. I know cold waters. I know Puget Sound. I don't know tropical waters. Oh my God, he saved my life. I would have been killed. I wouldn't be here this minute if it wasn't for Abu. Oh my God. I'm lucky to be alive.

Overcome with gratitude, I rushed to Abu to thank him, but every time I uttered, "Shukrun," which is the Arabic word for thank you, Abu deflected it, and continued with his merrymaking. I backed off.

Then Muhammad told me that it was strange that Abu knew the snake was going after me because I was snorkeling so far from shore I could hardly be seen, and the snake definitely could not have been seen with the naked eye.

In that moment I understood the entire scenario. Abu used his powerful, paranormal abilities to see the snake, and thus save my life. He had deflected my "thank you" because he didn't need to boast or brag. His motivation had not come from his ego. He killed the snake because saving another person's life was the natural, caring, and civilized thing to do.

I met Abu on the shores of the Red Sea in Sudan at a run-down resort called Arous where I spent my spring break. Arous had seen better days in a distant past when Sudan welcomed tourists, and Arous was a thriving resort frequented by vacationers who basked in Sudan's hot sun during the cold European winters. Those prosperous Sudanese days had long since passed, and the resort was in a state of increasing decay.

Abu was lean, tall, chocolate-brown, and devilishly handsome with a body as strong as iron. He was from the Hadendoa tribe which had been known for centuries for its fierceness in fighting.

Our guide told me, "His tribe speak ancient Hadendoa language, and Arabic. Hadendoa tribe people never tell real name to stranger. They believe bad luck. Abu Medino mean father of Medino. Abu mean father. Daughter of Abu, her name Medino."

My guess was that Abu was at least eighty, but he could have been fifty, or one-hundred. I really don't know. His dress, his stories, and his untroubled countenance were as timeless as the desert itself.

He slept next to his fire pit, in the open air, on a woven bed with split-wood bedsteads resting in the desert sand. Another man slept on the bare sand next to Abu's campfire. He was in his fifties, I think, and he was seemingly Abu's body guard. The other man was missing several teeth. His fuzzy, black hair stood on end and stuck straight out, about twelve inches in every direction. He was a representation of the Hadendoas whom the Brits nicknamed the Fuzzy Wuzzies. The Fuzzy Wuzzy chap wore a white jalabeya which is the traditional Sudanese garment, and a navy-blue vest.

I accepted Abu's invitation to spend three evenings sitting in the sand next to his charcoal-burning fire atop a hillside in back of the Arous guest cabins. There he shared his stories and his wisdom with me, into the wee hours of the morning. Since he did not speak English, this was translated through Muhammad.

Abu and I spent most of our time next to his campfire, but he did invite me for a brief time into his living quarters which amounted to a single room about twenty feet by twenty feet located inside of a long, narrow, empty cement building. In his room was an old bed with a drooping mattress, and two ancient trunks. While mice scampered up and down the walls, and mosquitoes circled and hummed around us, he lifted the creaky lids to the trunks, and carefully handed me photographs of him in his younger days standing next to smiling, tan, vibrant, shapely European women clad in skimpy bikinis. These photos were taken years ago when Arous thrived.

We walked outside again, and Abu hovered over his fire as he brewed extra-strong coffee in a traditional, orange-colored, clay coffee pot which he plucked with his bare hands from the embers. From that pot Abu, with instinctive dignity, poured his brew into a white demitasse cup for me. Half white sugar and half coffee, the mixture had the texture of mud. As we sat in the cold sand next to his campfire, which puffed white clouds of incense into the night air, we sipped our coffee and chewed snuff. Yes! Snuff! I really did chew snuff with Abu. How could I refuse his offer which came as naturally as offering a chair to a guest in a home in the United States. The snuff combined with the coffee made me dizzy and kind of nauseated, but I embraced the experience because it was so strange and different from anything I'd ever experienced before. For me, far-flung journeys are about opening to, and learning from, other realities. I was pleased as I felt myself releasing into a world very different from my own.

While a multitude of stars shone overhead in the night sky, Abu told stories from the days when he made lots of money smuggling camels from Sudan into Egypt, which Muhammad translated in broken English, "But that when he young and body could handle it." Abu talked about God, about beings of light, pure hearts, prophecies, and divination.

He also talked about shape-shifting. At this point in the conversation Muhammad, who had been doing his best to translate Abu's words, said to me, "I no understand nothings now. I saying words. I know words Abu saying, but I no understanding meaning of words. You understand? Only words to you? And why Abu tell you no repeat this stories? I no

3

understanding." The tone of Muhammad's voice was one of great frustration and slight disgust; he wasn't understanding a thing. The problem for Muhammad was that he had no background in the esoteric arts. Even though he could translate the vocabulary words, he did not understand the concepts in the stories he was telling me.

I, on the other hand, understood every word. I told Muhammad the following, "I understand enough to make me want to hear more. Keep translating, Muhammad." My purpose in saying this was twofold. I didn't want to give myself away and make Muhammad think I was some sort of weirdo, and I also dearly wanted Muhammad to keep on translating. Muhammad did continue to translate.

After what seemed to be about two hours of stories, Abu shifted from storytelling mode into ceremonial comportment. With the air of a high priest preparing sacred communion, he lifted an aged, rumpled, brown, burlap bag from his side. Out of this sanctified satchel he lifted several, small, sea-worn cowry shells, and he cast the shells onto the golden-brown sand. With Muhammad translating in his endearing, broken English, Abu read my fortune from the formation made by the shells. "Your mother no have sister. You no have communication with father. Your father have dark soul. You no have children." With that opening information he gained my initial trust because every word was true.

Muhammad continued translating, "You have pure heart. You protected by pure, white light from God. You leave this country soon and go on very long journey. You are going be very happy because you work hard resolve conflict in your personality. Your spirit one with Allah, with God. There no separation in your spirit from God, and your protection come from God, always."

With those words Abu gained my full trust because, once again, what he'd said was true. For example, soon I would be leaving Sudan for my summer vacation in Seattle and that would be a long journey.

Then Abu invited Muhammad and me to go fishing with him. The three of us hiked down a hillside, in relaxed silence, to a lagoon. We stood on the edge of the tranquil Red Sea with the quiet night surrounding us. Abu slipped off his jalabeya which was so old and worn it looked as if it were made of cobwebs. He waded into the water wearing only his underpants, a tank top, and his white turban on his head. As he set his line, he spoke in a soothing voice to the fish he was about to catch, and a memory stirred inside of me from my childhood. I remembered talking with eerily similar, soothing utterances to fish in Puget Sound when I was three, four, and five years old and fishing with my father in his sixteen-foot sport-fishing boat on the waters of Puget Sound.

When Abu emerged from the water, he stood beside me. I was wearing pants with long johns underneath, a turtleneck top and a warm jacket, and I was so cold I was shivering. After thirty minutes in the water Abu stood in the cool night air, wearing next to nothing, and he was not shivering at all.

It was then I decided Abu must be at least eighty years old, but when I asked him, through Muhammad, how old he was, he laughed and said, "Twenty-five!"

I thought, He definitely has the energy and vitality of a twenty-five-year-old.

We bade each other good night, and Abu turned towards the hillside and his open-air bedroom. Muhammad and I turned to go to our cabins.

The following morning I got up before dawn, did a photo shoot with a wild camel on the sand dunes at sunrise, walked back to my cabin, changed into my swim suit, and walked to the beach where I swam and snorkeled for hours. Later that afternoon, Abu draped the dead sea snake across his shoulders and across the shoulders of the children. While I watched them laugh and parade around the grounds of the resort, I learned I was alive, thanks to Abu.

Imbued with paranormal powers, humble, charming, upbeat, and generous, Abu is a mystical being who is rich in wisdom and life experience. Poor as a church mouse, he is a living lesson in true prosperity. Recognizing me as a kindred, reformed rascal and a sister in spirit, he opened his world and his heart to me. I owe him my life. How can I repay him? I can do the same for another some day.

Author's note: After I wrote this piece, I learned that deadly eels live in the Red Sea, but sea snakes do not. Therefore, what was referred to as a "sea snake" by the indigenous people must have been an eel.

Chapter 2

AIRPORT BLUES

Beware of Khartoum International Airport! If the airport workers' attitudes have not changed since I was there, I am here to tell you to be prepared for unavoidable hassles all of which are contrived on the spot. Above all, do not interpret your experience in the airport as an omen of your upcoming experience in Sudan. The airport experience represents the antithesis of the sweet Sudanese people.

I have come to dread the Khartoum airport, crawling with stone-faced soldiers dressed in forest-green, long-sleeved shirts with matching pants and berets, each carrying a machine gun slung over his tense shoulder. Their cold eyes dart around the large room, landing momentarily on Sudanese Muslims, Muslims from other countries, and infidels (such as me) with equal suspicion.

One of the teachers in my school summed up the situation when she said, "I swear they round up all the meanest jerks in this country and haul them to the Khartoum International Airport, dress them in army fatigues, stick a gun in their hands, and tell them to hassle people as much as they want to." Every country in the world has its meanies; it's just that here they all seem to be gathered together in the airport which gives them all the more power, and makes for an ordeal to get in and out of Sudan.

I can put up with the fact that there is no food and no drinkable water anywhere in the airport, no toilet paper in the stinky, squat toilet in the women's bathroom, and no air conditioning and it's usually about 115 degrees Fahrenheit. What gets to me are the meanies, and the constant bureaucratic disorganization and resulting rigmarole such as filling out long forms, and waiting in long lines especially if you are in possession of money from the United States.

Anyone with U. S. dollars has to declare, on paper, every single dollar upon entering Sudan. When you exit the country you have to produce those same declaration forms and the same amount of money. If you attempt to leave Sudan with more dollars than when you entered, I assure you that the extra dollars will be aggressively confiscated. I don't know what happens if you exit with fewer, but it can't be good.

Speaking for the women, prior to every departure you have to step inside a tiny cubicle where a black curtain is drawn by a stern Muslim woman. There you are frisked by that harsh female, and her technique is so thorough it borders on being perverted. My advice for all women is never to hide money in your brassiere when you leave Sudan because she will find it for sure. I've heard many stories of women being reduced to sobbing when their hidden money was discovered in their bra.

The problem for me is that whenever I am preparing to leave Sudan, I always have more money than when I arrived because my school pays me in U. S. dollars. My solution is to fold my one-hundred dollar U. S. bills into teeny-tiny squares, and cram them into the bottom of brown, plastic, vitamin containers with very narrow openings. I then jam those containers full of cotton balls. So far, so good. I haven't been caught and I feel smug, although I'm not proud of it, each time I successfully smuggle my U. S. dollars past the mean airport lady.

Case in point of a contrived hassle is the following Khartoum airport incident that happened to me when I was returning from the East African Teachers' Conference, followed by a short vacation on Zanzibar Island. The customs inspector spied my snorkel, grabbed it, thrust it high in the air above his head, and gave a signal to six guards with rifles. They surrounded me, and interrogated me for the next twenty tense minutes with menacing expressions and postures.

They pointed to my snorkel and snarled, "What you use this for?"

I said, "I use it for swimming."

They said, "Fimming? What you mean 'fimming?'" The implication was that fimming was irrevocably sinful.

7

I said, "Not fimming. Swimming."

They asked me over and over in demanding voices, "What you use this for?"

I told the truth, "To see fish."

Eyeing me with immense suspicion they asked, in broken English, "Why you want see fish?"

They seemed to be convinced that my snorkel was either to be used as the makings of a pipe bomb or else it was some kind of sex toy. They continued to express great displeasure with my answers. Their interrogation went around in useless circles, on and on, and on. Eventually they let me proceed through the customs line.

Yet another humongous hassle occurred one fateful August 9th. I had just returned to Khartoum from my summer break in Seattle. I'd been standing in line in 120 degree heat for an hour, and I needed a drink of water. I unscrewed the top of my quart-size nalgene container, and I began sipping water. Six soldiers, one with a machine gun, surrounded me and began a snarly interrogation which proceeded like this, "You have drink? What in bottle? You have drink!"

Those bullies were insinuating that I was drinking an illicit alcoholic beverage (which I would never do because by law Sudan is a dry country). I offered the container to the guys so they could smell it, but they recoiled in disgust. Desperately wanting to put an end to this interrogation, I talked to them in Arabic, saying, "Malesh. Moya."

What my words meant were, It's time to move on. This is only water.

However, the soldiers did not believe it was time to move on. Finally, I extended my hand to them, with the water container in my hand, and motioned to them that they could empty the contents of my container onto the floor. They backed off, but that wasn't the end of it. The head guy assigned three of his soldiers to follow me, and glower at me, until I exited the airport.

Another example of a big hassle happened when, upon handing my handwritten, required, exit form to an uncompromising man at the exit counter, I was told curtly, "Writing messy! We cannot read! Fill out different form. Go there!" I went to where he pointed, only to discover they were no more blank forms. Uh huh, I thought, Catch 22. I returned to the guy who had spoken curtly to me and I asked him for another blank form. He was gloating and sneering as he referred me to a line that had about fifty people in it. If I had gotten into that line, I would have missed my plane because the line was moving so slowly. I quickly took stock of the situation, and then surreptitiously cut into the front of a different line where there was a relatively mild-mannered airline employee from whom I obtained a blank form. I then filled it out, and handed it to the difficult guy who, this time, let me proceed to the line for my airplane.

I don't take the hassles personally, and I'm not the only one who dreads the airport. The Sudanese have told me that they, too, get harassed. The Khartoum airport is the great equalizer because Sudanese, and foreigners, white skin and dark skin and every shade in between, we all get equally hassled there.

Don't be dissuaded about Sudan at the airport. The best is yet to come.

Chapter 3

AMERICAN CLUB

I frequent the fairly grimy American Club because it is the only place in this roasting-hot desert town where I can swim in a decent-sized swimming pool. It's fifty-meters long, to be exact. My American friend Ellie and I walk to the club a couple of times a week. It takes us about forty minutes to get there.

The club also serves food, and sometimes it's quite tasty. One afternoon, a few days before our American Thanksgiving, I was quite hungry after swimming laps for forty-five minutes. I ordered the American Club Lunch Special which I ate while sitting in the shade of a bamboo umbrella. The special included a generous portion of tender, oven-roasted turkey with gravy, mashed potatoes with fresh dill sprinkled on top, a scrumptious beet salad, zesty peanut soup, melt-in-your-mouth whip-cream chocolate cake for desert, and Turkish coffee with sugar and cardamom. All that food was only 5,000 Sudanese dinars which is the equivalent of about $3.00 in U. S. money.

For less than a dollar you can order a large pitcher of delicious, freshly-squeezed grapefruit juice or orange juice, which is a nice treat in this sweltering desert.

I've decided to look past the fact that the club never has toilet paper in the musty-smelling bathrooms, the floor tiles are cracked and uneven, and sometimes the pool looks rather bug infested. The choice is to come to the club, exercise in the pool, and then relax; or, sit at home. I've never been one to sit for long.

Ellie and I usually take a taxi home from the American Club. Sometimes, another club patron will offer us a ride home. During one of those rides home I had a stimulating conversation with the Sudanese man who was driving. He asked me if I liked Sudan and I told him, "Yes, I really like it here because the people are so friendly and relaxed. I have never experienced such friendly, kind, gentle, generous, and relaxed people. And they take the time to really care about each other. This is such a welcome relief from life in the United States where almost everyone seems to be quite stressed."

He laughed and said, "Yes, but they can be that friendly and relaxed here because they don't have any stress in their lives. Do you know how many hours a day a Sudanese person works? Two! We drink tea, we talk to each other, we talk on the phone, and on a good day we get about two hours of work done. And that's why we're one of the poorest countries in the world and why America is on top."

I laughed and said, "But, we're way too stressed, and we're working way too hard in my homeland. I think we all need to strike a balance point. We need to take the best from both of our cultures, and we all need to learn from each other, and change. Change for the better."

Chapter 4

ANCESTRAL
SCOTTISH BRIDGE

One afternoon I learned a new, mind-boggling fact about one of the bridges that transports vehicles and people across the Nile River. I'd travelled across that bridge countless times since my arrival in Khartoum, but never with a guide. That day some friends and I had hired a guide to take us to the camel market on the other side of town, and thus we had the guide's explanations. While we were crossing over the bridge, our guide explained, "This is a secondhand bridge. This bridge was brought from Edinburgh, Scotland, to Khartoum in the 1920s."

What really blew my mind is the fact that my maternal grandfather and his parents would have travelled across this same bridge when it was in Edinburgh, Scotland.

My grandfather was born in Outerson, Scotland, in 1893. When he was five years old he moved to Edinburgh with his parents. My Scottish great-grandparents and my grandfather would never, in their wildest imagination, have guessed that their great-granddaughter and granddaughter (me!) would, on a 130-degree day in the far future, travel over the same bridge in Khartoum, Sudan, that they travelled across in their native Scotland.

This puts a new spin on the old saying: everything changes, everything is connected, pay attention.

Chapter 5

ARCHEOLOGICAL SOCIETY FIELD TRIP

The Sudan Archaeological Society consists of a cross-cultural mishmash of about thirty Brits, Germans, Americans, Greeks, and sometimes a few Sudanese. Our outings are discontinued in the hot season, and resume when the weather cools down to an average daytime temperature of 110 degrees Fahrenheit. This proves to me that one's attitude about hot and cool temperatures, along with everything in life for that matter, is all relative.

We'd set out on this all-day fieldtrip on a chartered bus which was devoid of air conditioning, devoid of a bathroom, and devoid of comfortable seats. We rumbled through the congested, cement streets of downtown Khartoum lined with cement apartment buildings, cement houses, and cement office buildings, none of which were over five stories high. Within no time we had progressed onto dirt streets with square-shaped, adobe-looking houses surrounded by walls made of bricks. (The bricks, by the way, began as red mud which was shaped into blocks, dried outdoors in the baking sun, and then used to make houses and walls.) The houses and population became more sparse in no time at all. After about an hour of traveling we saw only flat, reddish-brown desert dotted with sheep wagging their long tails behind them, goats, small dwellings made of goat skins, and camels. After another thirty minutes, or so, there was nothing but desert, camels, and a meager scattering of scrawny acacia trees. Not one of those trees had more than a couple of handfuls of small, green leaves on it.

Our hodgepodge of Archeological Society members was quite a sight in that bus. There we were, a bunch of city dwellers, dripping with sweat, cooped up on a rusty, old bus. Our driver hightailed it at fifty miles an hour across the flat, gravelly, rust-colored desert blasting his horn. The windows and door were wide open, tattered and faded-blue window curtains billowed, and dust swirled inside and outside the bus. The bus bounced, lurched, creaked, groaned, whined, smoked and smelled as if it were going to catch on fire or blow up.

Several times we were lost. I always knew we were lost, again, when the bus driver swerved off our makeshift, sandy, desert road and careened across the rocky desert until he met up with tire tracks. He'd turn onto that improvised road and follow those tire tracks until they petered out, and thus it was time to search for more, fresh tire tracks to follow.

On many occasions, I thought our driver was to going to crash the bus into cute, wild, wide-eyed, baby camels that, deciding we were worth a long look, halted their desert meanderings squarely in front of our bus. There they stood, staring at us, while the bus driver, not slowing down an iota, blasted his horn nonstop. Each time, at the last second, the baby camel would veer out of our way.

Four hours after we boarded the bus, we rumbled to a halt beside an enormous mound of large boulders--called a jebel in Arabic--in the middle of an immense, flat desert that stretched as far as the eye could see. The Archeological Society affiliates piled out of the rusty bus, and gathered beside a remarkable boulder on which was carved a scene with a twenty-foot-tall figure wearing an Egyptian-looking headdress holding a stalk of sorghum to honor a sun god. Our guide told us the carving was made in the year 1 B.C. Slaves bowed at the foot of that figure, and more figures were depicted tumbling off a rock cliff presumably in a self-sacrifice to their god. Other boulders had etchings of giraffes, which indicated that in the year 1 B.C. there was enough water to support giraffes on this part of the planet. Now the surrounding desert is bone dry and there are no animals of any type with the exception of camels.

After the archeological explanation was finished, many in our group charged off on an impromptu rock-climbing expedition to the top of the jebel. Since I do not adore rock climbing I, along with another teacher, took off on a hike around the base of the jebel. It must have been at least 105 degrees and I was all too glad that the boulders shaded us from the sun during part of our walk.

Two or three hours later, my friend and I had completed our circumnavigation of the base of the jebel. We had returned to our starting point, but our bus was nowhere to be seen. It had vanished. Just then two male nomads, dressed in jalabeyas and navy-blue vests, appeared and they motioned for us to follow them. I thought, What the heck! Why not!

I hoped for the best and I prayed like mad that the worst didn't happen.

I followed them, scrambling up and over a large pile of rocks. Next, I had to bend down and crawl under some boulders. When I was standing again, much to my astonishment, the nomads pointed to several, ancient, ochre-colored paintings of cattle with long horns. Those paintings looked almost exactly like the paintings in that famous cave at Lascaux in Dordogne, France. I yelled to my friend to join me. Fearing the worst, she'd kept her distance from these two nomadic characters, and refused to follow them. Upon hearing my decidedly ecstatic yelling, she joined me and, standing in the welcoming shade of the boulders, she and I stared, speechless, at those stunning paintings from long, long ago.

The two nomads maintained a polite distance of about fifteen feet as they stared, speechless, at me. To them I must have looked like I had dropped in from another planet. On my legs I was sporting flamingo-pink, ankle-length, skin-tight cotton tights. I was also wearing a flamingo-pink billed cap, large pink sunglasses, and a midthigh length, Save the Manatees T-shirt, with a real-life photograph of a manatee swimming amongst tropical, pink coral across my breasts. I'm laying odds that these guys did not know that manatees exist on our planet. I am certain that these Sahara-dwelling Muslim men had never seen anything bearing even the slightest resemblance to the likes of me, or my attire, ever before.

After a few minutes I reached into my backpack, pulled out a fresh grapefruit, and handed it to one of the nomads as a way to say, Thank you. He was as pleased as a child with a new, plastic toy from an upscale department store. After he finished inspecting it, he placed it in the pocket of his navy-blue vest.

You might be wondering about my flashy, pink outfit. So, I think that this is a good place for me to add that, both in my classroom as well as whenever I am in the presence of Muslims in Khartoum, I wear conservatively colored ankle-length skirts and baggy tops. When I venture into the desert for a daytrip I almost always wear a relatively conservative outfit I describe in the chapter titled "Saving My Skin." However, on this particular day I knew I'd be driven in a friend's private car to and from the Archeological Society bus. On that bus I knew there would be exclusively Western Europeans. On that day, I was in the mood to bust out and be me and I decided to wear one of my distinctly "me" outfits. Thus, I sported the flamingo-pink garb the day of this outing.

My friend and I then wandered around the area looking for our bus. We came upon it about a half mile from where it had dropped us off, sitting atop a hillside. We learned that the bus did not have a working ignition, and thus the driver always had to park it at the top of a slope so he could start it on compression. Our bus conundrum was answered, but I bet that those bewildered desert dwellers are still puzzling over me and my hot-pink Save the Manatees apparel.

Chapter 6

BARGAINING FOR PRODUCE ON CEMETERY ROAD

Once or twice a week Mr. Yaqub, my after-school taxi driver, dutifully parks his beat-up, yellow, mini-size, station-wagon taxi next to one of many farmers' trucks parked alongside Cemetery Road where I bargain for my fruits and vegetables.

My school is located at the south end of Cemetery Road and the farmers, who are also the produce vendors, are located at the north end. So, it's logical for us to stop here on my way home from school. Since I buy my produce next to the cemetery itself, I'll take a paragraph to describe it. It's of interest because it is very different from ours in the United States.

In this typical cemetery there are no adornments of any type. No fancy tombstones, no flowers. Most of the graves are marked with thin, small, rectangular, gray headstones approximately twelve inches by six inches. The cemetery grounds are filled with unadulterated, brownish-yellow, sandy dirt. The graves are of two types. Either they are shallow, or the body has been placed on top of the dirt and a mound of sandy dirt has been shoveled over the body. It's been explained to me that some of the graves are not marked to avoid an enemy putting the evil eye on the deceased.

Mr. Yaqub parks his beat-up taxi next to one of the farmer's trucks. (Incidentally, all of the farmers' trucks are white Toyota pickup trucks. They are white because white reflects the intense sun. I don't know why they are all Toyotas.) Then Mr. Yaqub helps me pick out my fruits and vegetables which are piled in the back of one of the trucks.

The variety of produce is more limited in the hot months simply because it's so very hot. Also, the quality isn't up to par because both the vendors and their produce spend the entire day outside without any type of refrigeration, and the daytime temperatures are a minimum of 120 degrees Fahrenheit in the shade. I repeat, in the shade.

Mr. Yaqub always puffs on a cigarette in the background while I stand and sweat in the sweltering sun and sputter phrases of Arabic to the vendor.

Arabic is a difficult language for me. Everything about it is foreign including the sentence structures, gender-specific verb conjugations, and sounds. When I make the Arabic sounds I have to wake up parts of my tongue and throat that have been asleep my entire life. When I shop I practice twisting my tongue around some basic and necessary Arabic words and phrases, such as "portucan nus kilo" (a half kilo of oranges) and "asswad hamsajamil" (five pretty eggplant). At some point I ask, "Becum?" (How much?) After the farmer's reply, I always deliver the expected protest, "Kida katir!" (This is too much!) meaning that the price is too high and needs to lowered in order for the sale to be made.

Mr. Yaqub fusses in the background about the price being too high and if the vendor doesn't lower the price he'll make the sale but kill the customer, meaning that he will sell his goods but the customer won't return. After some huffing, sighing, and eye-rolling, the farmer always lowers the price. When the bargaining is over, the farmer from whom I purchased my produce, as well as all the farmer-vendors who are within earshot, all smile and compliment me on my Arabic and encourage me to speak more Arabic. The more I speak, the more they smile, and the more free produce they give to me to acknowledge and encourage my efforts at speaking their beloved language. This, of course, encourages me to speak more and more. It's a fun and rewarding stage on which to practice my marketplace Arabic. The farmers are good teachers. They make learning fun and rewarding.

The produce vendors, as well as all the shopkeepers in Khartoum along with all the customers in the shops, always go out of their way to help me speak Arabic. The Sudanese listen to every sound I utter. They gently correct my pronunciation and applaud, literally, my attempts at speaking Arabic. From the perspective of a teacher, I can say that they are effective teachers because they provide a positive atmosphere where I enjoy practicing my burgeoning foreign language.

Chapter 7

BEGGARS AND
ALLAH KAREEM

I encounter street beggars on a daily basis because I don't have a car and I walk almost everywhere. All of my grocery shopping for prepackaged items is done in a series of hole-in-the-wall stores. I walk or take a taxi to get to the vicinity of those shops, and then I travel on foot between them. (For the record, there is one supermarket in Khartoum, but it's located far away on the other side of town and their prices there are sky-high. So I never shop there.)

I clearly remember my first grocery shopping foray in Khartoum. Beggars were frequently at my side including an aged, withered man with a deformed leg and several small children holding gray, metal bowls in which to collect money. My teacher-friend Patty, who had volunteered to show me where to shop, said to me, "Just say to them 'Allah kareem' because that means 'God is generous' or 'God is good,' and after you say that to the beggars they leave."

So, I tried saying it, and the beggars left. I've used it ever since. The beggars here are starving, but they're not aggressive unlike every other country I've lived in, and that includes the United States.

I always feel uncomfortable and vulnerable when I am in the middle of a gang of child beggars and my heart goes out to them, but I never give money to them. Not giving money to beggars is one of the most difficult disciplines I've held myself to. I've held to it because no matter how much money you give to them it's never enough, and you can't control what they spend their money on. Sometimes the money goes to quick highs, and I have witnessed child beggars sniffing glue on the streets of Khartoum. Also, I've been told that the Sudanese beggars learn where you live, and they come to your house and beg relentlessly from you, and they bring all their beggar friends to your house, and they come back for more and more. I don't know if this is true, but I don't want to risk it happening to me. Most important, giving money to a beggar does nothing to solve the problem.

A few days ago, a friend and I were walking down a street and we were surrounded by a pack of barefoot, grimy, sweaty, beggar children wearing rags. They were pushing against us and whimpering, "Baksheesh," (which translates as spare change). They wouldn't leave after we said, "Allah kareem." So, my friend and I had to be patient and wait for a car to approach us. Whenever I, or any foreigner for that matter, am surrounded by beggars who won't leave, the first car that drives by with male occupants always stops. The occupants in that car get out and graciously, but firmly, tell the children to leave. The men then wait until the children leave before they drive off. I always tell the men an earnest, "Shukrun!" which means, Thank you! The men always apologize on behalf of the beggars before they climb into their car and leave.

I have travelled and lived in many countries in the world and I have never before encountered this custom of protecting foreigners from beggars. On the rare occasions when "Allah kareem" doesn't work, I sincerely appreciate this act of protection and caring.

Chapter 8

BULL WHIPS AND SUDANESE ROCKERS

"There could be big trouble," Ali said with intense seriousness as he tried to dissuade my European friend, Fatima, and me from going to the rock-and-roll concert. He continued, "Women do not go to these concerts. It is not good for women to be seen at such occasions. Foreign women do not ever go to such events."

Fatima and I insisted, saying, "We want to go. We want to experience a Sudanese rock concert."

What could Ali do? In keeping with his Sudanese good-host values, he complied with our request to attend the concert.

At 7 p.m. we paid the price of admission which was the equivalent of U. S. $3.50 and we made our way into the jam-packed, standing-room-only concert grounds filled with approximately 2,000 Sudanese men, and fifteen Sudanese women. Yes, I counted the women, all of whom had their heads covered with large scarves. Judging by the overtly sexual, seductive, and lewd body language of those fifteen women, I'm laying odds that all of them were seasoned prostitutes.

I was the only white person in the audience, and the only woman without a headscarf. To say I stuck out like a sore thumb is an understatement.

The opening act was in progress when we entered the concert. It was festival seating, but there was not one vacant chair to sit on. Since Ali's cousin was the lead guitarist, Ali decided that the three of us should push our way to the area where the band members were sitting because he was sure that they would give us their chairs. We pressed through the crowd and three of the band members, being Sudanese gentlemen, gave us their chairs. They went on stage shortly thereafter.

We picked up the vacated chairs, and began to wriggle our way through the crowd toward the stage so we could see the show. When we were quite close to the stage, we were met by twenty policemen who were dressed in green, army fatigues. Each carried a bullwhip in his right hand. The officers gathered together to form a line, and they began to advance towards us while slapping their bullwhips against the ground. The three of us had inadvertently crossed into an off-limits area, and we were too close to the stage. The police wore menacing expressions on their faces and they meant business! Fatima, Ali, and I did an immediate about-face and turned towards the audience.

Unbeknownst to us, the entire audience had been following our every move. All 2,000 concertgoers were laughing, smiling, and pointing at us. No one was watching the rock band. Everyone was watching the three of us and the twenty policemen who had now retreated only because the three of us had retreated. But, all twenty pairs of police eyes were fixed on us, and their bodies were tense with adrenalin. Just then, one large section of the audience stood up, and began shuffling around and rearranging their broken-down, metal, card-table chairs. With much to-do a space big enough for three people and three chairs was cleared, and the audience beckoned us to come on in! Several men made their way out of the crowded audience to where we were standing, and courteously carried Fatima's and my chairs fifty yards to the cleared area. Fatima and I, laughing and smiling, followed the men. Everyone we passed, or tripped over, said a cheerful, enthusiastic, and loud, "Welcome!" to Fatima and me.

We had upstaged the opening act.

I couldn't bear to turn around and look at Ali. I figured that he must have been praying for mercy from these two, rapscallion, Westernized women. During the concert every time my focus left the performers--and I frequently lost my focus because the sound system was bad and the music sounded fuzzy and crackly, and it faded in and out--as I looked one way or the other, there were hundreds of eyes looking at me as I swayed my body and snapped my fingers in time to the music.

After the concert was over a four-year-old Sudanese boy walked up to me, stationed himself in front of me, and stared at me for five minutes. Both of his brown eyes and his mouth were wide-open as he studied me from head to toe, and toe to head. He looked as if he were encountering an alien. I'm certain he'd never before seen a person with white skin and brown-blond hair. He continued to stare at me up and down, over and over, until his father collected him in his arms and whisked him away.

Like it or not, everywhere I go in Khartoum I am a spectacle.

Chapter 9

BUS RIDES WITH
THE LOCALS

The first bus I boarded, during my first and last day of riding buses in Khartoum, hurtled in the direction of downtown Khartoum with Sudanese pop music blaring at ear-splitting decibels from the bus driver's portable stereo system. The pink fringe framing the front window of the bus jangled as the entire busload of brown-skinned passengers stared at me. I was only white person on the crowded bus, the only woman dressed in a Western-style white blouse and a black-and-pink floral-print A-line skirt, and the only woman without a head covering. All the other women were dressed in traditional tobes made of brightly-colored fabric. Some of the men wore Western trousers and T-shirts, but most were wearing traditional, white jalabeyas and crocheted skullcaps.

I'd waited for that bus on Africa-Airport Road at a very dusty intersection not far from my apartment where dozens of red-and-white buses, white trucks, and white cars stopped to drop off and pick up their passengers in clouds of dust.

After ten minutes of standing and waiting, I heard Maha's familiar, strong, friendly voice yelling my name from inside a bus. I boarded that bus and plunked myself down in the seat next to Maha, which she had saved for me. She and I exchanged the standard greeting between two women in Sudan, simultaneous kisses on each others' right cheeks, followed by simultaneous kisses on each others' left cheeks, followed by simultaneous kisses on each others' right cheeks. A total of three kisses given to and from each woman.

Maha, my Sudanese friend, had taken it upon herself to teach me how to take buses in Khartoum because it would save me a lot of money according to Sudanese standards. Up to this point I had been walking, or taking taxis which are much more expensive than the bus.

I had several questions to ask Maha including: since the destination and number are written on the bus in Arabic, and I can barely speak Arabic much less read it, how will I ever know which bus is my bus? Next question: How can I figure out when to give my money? I've watched the guys who collect the bus fares as they lean out the door of the bus, snap their fingers, and expect bus riders to give them their bus money. But, it's only after x number of snaps that you give your money and I can't, for the life of me, figure out the rhythm of the snap system. The clothes and appearance of the money collector are that of the average man on the street. So, my next question is: How can I know if the money-taker guy is a legitimate bus employee or just some guy who is trying to bilk me out of my bus money? All of my questions were unanswerable due to the language barrier coupled with my total lack of cultural bus-riding knowledge.

Maha and I waited for, and boarded, a total of three buses that day and I cannot tell you how many times my body was jostled, bumped, pushed, whacked, and elbowed, and how many times my sandal-clad feet were stomped on by Sudanese women wearing spiky, high heels who were stampeding in hordes to catch their buses. The Sudanese are not gentle when it comes to catching buses. It isn't as if there are not many buses in Khartoum, quite the opposite. There are scads of buses. However, due to the law of supply and demand the buses are always chock-full and it's first come, first served.

The price difference between buses and taxis amounts to only a couple of dollars in U. S. currency. Taxis are expensive for Sudanese, but inexpensive for me, thankfully. As colorful as local bus rides are, and as much as I appreciate Maha's offer to help me, I've decided that I'm going to continue to take taxis.

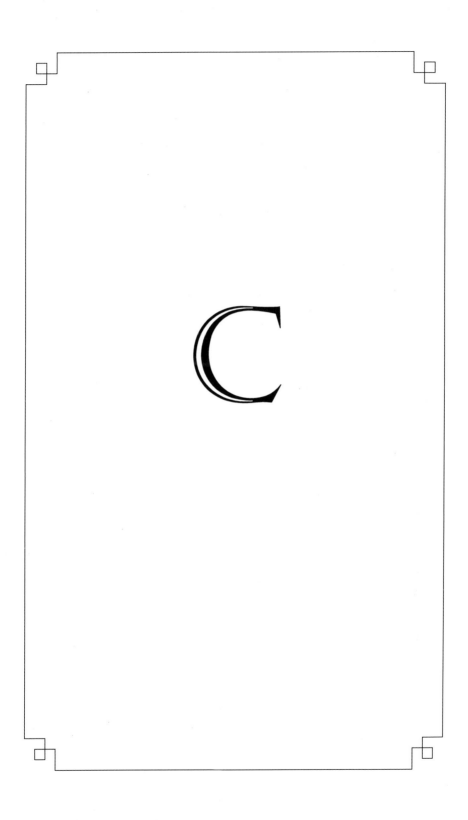

Chapter 10

CHAOTIC STREETS

This is the most confusing and disorienting city I have ever lived in, and that includes several cities around the world. There are no familiar ways for me to orient myself. There are precious few street signs, no mountains, and no tall buildings. The tallest man-made structures are the slender minarets which stand alongside the main buildings of the mosques and from which the call to prayer emanates. Living here makes me understand why, long ago, people thought the earth was flat. Khartoum is situated in the middle of a flat, flat, flat desert and if you didn't know better, it would be easy to think that the whole world is flat from the vantage point of Khartoum. Unless I look at the sun or moon, I never know if I'm going north, south, east, or west and neither does anybody else. It seems that everyone navigates by landmarks because there is no other way to navigate around here.

A few streets do have names posted in Arabic, but this doesn't help me because I can't read Arabic. To add to the confusion, many of the streets do have numbers, but rarely is a number posted. Somehow you get to know, and memorize, the numbers of the streets that do have numbers, but no houses or apartments have numbers.

In an attempt to orient myself when I first arrived, I naively tried to locate a map of Khartoum. I soon discovered that there is no map of Khartoum in existence. I asked everyone I met including a real estate agent for a map of Khartoum, and I was told that there isn't one. I suppose this is true because you can't map something that doesn't exist, and since most streets are unnamed you can't put them on a map.

Everyone in Khartoum drives crazily, but relatively slowly, thank God, because of the poor condition of the streets and roads which are crooked and made of dust-producing red desert dirt. They are filled with ruts and large holes, as well as countless potholes which are big enough to swallow a car and its passengers forever. All roads are strewn with rocks which are treacherous to the tires. The drivers do make up for lost time on the paved thoroughfares, of which there are approximately five, where they whiz along at nerve-racking speed.

All of these rutted and bumpy roads are filled with hundreds of wandering, brown-white-and-black shaggy-fur goats with long, floppy ears. Weaving in, out, and around the goats are swarms of rattletrap cars driven by men, and by lead-footed mamas wearing colorful headscarves.

There are thousands of little, two-wheeled, wooden carts in the middle of, as well as along the sides of, the streets. Every donkey is whipped by a man who is sitting in the cart and is dressed in a white turban and a flowing, white gown called a jalabeya. A jalabeya is always white, mid-calf length, A-line and made of cotton with a scoop neck or V-neck and it is the traditional dress for Sudanese men. Most of the men wear this white gown, and it wafts in the relentless desert wind.

Flatbed trucks rumble down the streets loaded with freshly picked produce such as sweet bananas, juicy oranges and grapefruit, bright red tomatoes, purple eggplants, mint, and small green limes. Both men and women hang onto the sides of the trucks for dear life or they sit next to or smack-dab on top of the vegetables and fruits. My first couple of days here I lived in mortal fear of seeing people being thrown off the trucks and crushed dead in front of my eyes; that hasn't happened so far, and I hope it doesn't ever happen.

Rickety taxis shimmy down the crowded streets. All taxis are small, battered and orangish-yellow, are individually owned, and in various states of great disrepair. Shock absorbers are nonexistent and wheel suspension is unheard of. Taxi drivers honk their horns while they dart around other taxis shimmying at a slower pace than their taxi.

I can only hope that my taxi doesn't hit one of the wandering goats. As we dodge the goats I pray we don't smack into any number of people who crisscross and jaywalk the streets every which way. I also hope a tire doesn't fall off and send my taxi careening into scads of other nearby, wobbly taxis. In the meantime, I keep myself distracted and amused as I gawk at the taxi's interior customized by each driver-owner.

Taxi interiors reek of tacky, and I delight in these decorations as an expression of folk art. Brightly sequined veils drape across the top of windshields. Plastered on taxi windows are garish decals of brilliant-blue doves, fat golden lions, smiley-faced cartoon characters with brown skin, palm trees and beach scenes with cartoon surfers and letters that spell Hawan. I figured that Hawan must be some kind of fancy way of spelling Hawaiian in a pidgin mixture of Hawaiian, English, and Arabic. My favorite taxi had decals of bright-red hearts and bright-red capital letters that spelled LOVE, and Sudanese pop music blared from loud speakers positioned directly behind the back of my head. Every time that driver stomped on his brakes, which was not often enough on that wild ride, the music turned off and a computerized nee-nee-nee-nee sound blared at the same time as red lights flashed on and off across the dashboard. That taxi was also battered, rickety, and orangish-yellow and it, too, shimmied down the street.

I'm frequently picked up by taxi drivers who have long, deep scars on their cheeks; that's because every Sudanese tribe has its own, unique, scarring pattern. The scarring is done as a rite of passage, but the custom is dying out as Sudan, along with the rest of the world, is becoming increasingly westernized.

The rate of literacy in Sudan is very low, and hardly any taxi driver can read or write. If you can't communicate with them in spoken Arabic, you have to be a decent-enough artist to draw a picture of where you want them to take you. I'm a lousy artist, but Ashraf, my Arabic teacher, is talented and he drew a picture for me to show to all taxi drivers; it's of a famous and thus very recognizable mosque which stands at the end of my street. All I have to do is show Ashraf's drawing to a taxi driver, and he takes me to that mosque. From there, I simply need to walk one block to get to my apartment. That drawing works like a charm, every time.

Since the streets aren't named, people give the streets a fitting name and everyone seems to know what everyone else is talking about. For example, another teacher and I frequently take a forty-five minute walk to buy barbecued chicken on a street we named Chicken Street because that particular dirt street is lined with tiny restaurants with huge grills out in front. Every grill billows white smoke, and is packed with pieces of barbequing chicken which have been marinated in the restaurant's special, spicy sauce. Another good example is a street in Omdurman, the old section of Khartoum, named Street 40. It's the street where the camel drivers set out on their treks across the desert to Egypt, and it takes 40 days to make that desert crossing.

Adding to the overall confusion are thousands of empty, plastic grocery bags blowing every which way, up, down, and across the streets every minute of every day and night.

In the midst of all of this confusion, muggings and rape are unheard of, and I've never seen or heard of a civilian carrying a gun or a knife. The biggest street-crime news I ever heard was a report about a big, society wedding held at the large mosque that sits at the end of my street. As the wedding was taking place, three thieves stole forty pairs of shoes that had respectfully been placed outside the front entrance to the mosque by the wedding attendees. Evidently a long chase ensued, and the garbage sacks containing all forty pairs of shoes were recovered. This was big news in Khartoum.

I do appreciate feeling safe along with being thoroughly entertained every time I step out of my front door. Every day on the streets is a colorful, creative carnival of unfettered, cacophonous life fashioned without concern for orchestrated sophistication.

Chapter 11

CLOSE ENCOUNTERS
WITH CAMELS

Take a quick minute to picture how you would react if you saw a camel tied up in front of a building in the downtown section of your city. I laughed with delight one afternoon when a friend drove me into downtown Khartoum where I spied a large, light-brown, one-humped camel tied securely in front of an office building.

Camels tickle me and I do love seeing them in Khartoum. So, I'm now going to tell you several of my first-hand Khartoum camel stories.

Not only are camels tied up in the downtown section of the city, but one strolls by my living room window about once a week or so. Yes! In front of my living room window. I know the camel has arrived whenever I hear the familiar, singsong voice of the Sudanese merchant announcing in his smooth, rhythmic chant that he is selling the goods that he has packed inside of the bulging saddle bags which are slung across the camel's hump. The peddler is always dressed in an ironed and starched, bright-white jalabeya, and a white skullcap as he leads his beige camel down the middle of the street in front of my house. I've always wondered what he is selling. I've never seen anyone on my street buy anything from him, and there has never been anyone in sight who speaks English when the man shows up with his camel. Since there hasn't been any way to find out what he's selling, I've had fun conjuring up all kinds of interesting possibilities in my mind.

One sunny afternoon I was transfixed at the sight of two camels on the sandy banks of the Nile River. My Arabic teacher had invited me to go to a party that he and his college friends were having at a beach named Nassir. There were lots of people enjoying a day at the beach, and the scene was similar to a U.S. beach scene in as much as jeeps had been driven out to the water's edge, and there were playful water fights with guys laughing as they threw each other into the water. There were also some noticeable differences between Nassir and a U.S. beach. Even though it was a scorching-hot day all the men were wearing long pants and the women were wearing skirts, and not one of the women was in the water. The biggest difference of all was a man who wandered by with his two camels in tow. Have you ever seen a man with camels lollygagging along a beach? I hadn't. I walked toward them to get a closer look. I stood still for about fifteen minutes marveling at the sight of the two camels. When I was ready to rejoin my friends, I turned around and discovered that about eighty Sudanese people had gathered in a silent semicircle in the white sand, and they were intently watching me watching the camels. I was as captivating to those Sudanese people as the camels were to me. What one deems as exotic depends on one's cultural context.

Need a pick-me-up from the doldrums of humdrum life? I recommend attending a camel race. I found it hilarious. One afternoon a friend invited me to go to the camel races which were held on the same afternoon as the horse races, at a stadium on the outskirts of downtown Khartoum. The expat European patrons in the audience watched the staid horse races, and paid no attention whatsoever to the camel races. For me, the disciplined horse events paled in comparison to the unpredictable behavior of the lanky camels. Each long-legged camel would lope down the track in a straight line for an indeterminate amount of time. Then, out of the blue, they'd stretch their long, flexible necks and swerve their bodies randomly to one side or the other of the track while bumping into, or cutting off, other camels who then began swerving into other camels. This caused the camels' jockey-owners, who were boys between the ages of ten and fourteen dressed in traditional, flowing, white jalabeyas, to go nuts whipping their camels, but to no avail. Right before my eyes was the manifestation of a magnificent, impromptu, crazy, camel dance choreographed on the spot by one of the most obstreperous and independent creatures on the planet. As far as I'm concerned, you couldn't ask for more on a day at the races.

Now it's time for some camel-riding advice. Take it from me, if you ever ride a camel remember this: when the camel is both getting up from the ground and going down to let you off, you must not look down at the ground. In other words, when the camel lifts up from its knees, and when it sits down again, you must look straight ahead. If you do not do this, you will most likely be thrown off the camel; the reason being that camels dip way forward both when they are in the process of standing up and when they are in the process of sitting down. A friend kindly imparted this advice to me in a Sudanese nomad camp immediately before I went on my first camel ride. Most foreigners don't know this vital tidbit about camels and there are many stories about foreigners getting thrown headfirst into the desert, airborne. Consider yourself forewarned. It's a simple technique and it works.

Since there are so many camels in Khartoum and Sudan, there must be a camel market, right? Right! Some friends and I hired a bus and a guide to take us there, and the following is a glimpse into the biggest camel market in Khartoum. The market is located on the outskirts of town, about an hour's drive from my apartment. The following present-tense vignette is taken directly from the notes I wrote during our trip to the Khartoum camel market.

Our first stop is a camel barbeque. We get off our bus and walk along a brown, dirt alleyway winding through a local market. Small shops line the pathway on either side. After ten minutes of walking, we arrive at the barbeque joint. We sit on rickety chairs which are set up in the dirt under a roof which looks as if it will collapse at any second. Barbequed camel is served to us along with plates of roasted vegetables. Clouds of black flies descend, and swarm all over the vegetables. I opt to eat camel meat only.

After about fifteen minutes, I am still chewing the same piece of camel meat. I maneuver the wad into the side of my cheek and, hamming it up, I say in a very loud voice, "Hey everybody! How's the camel chewing gum?" My friends laugh and laugh because their camel cuisine experience matches mine. But, I must say, the semi-gamey, mostly bland, and terribly greasy camel meat serves a very useful purpose. It leaves a thick layer of oil on my tender lips and this protects them from the parching heat and strong wind.

We walk back to our bus. Our next stop is the camel market.

After a short ride I see nothing but flat, brown desert filled with about two thousand, light-brown, one-humped, tethered camels. Smiling men dressed in jalabeyas mill around the camels. Many more men sit in pickup trucks or Mercedes sedans. Since a Mercedes costs as much in Sudan as it does abroad, this gives me a good clue about the lucrative nature of the camel selling-and-buying business. Our guide tells us that most of the camels are being bought and sold for export to Egypt and Libya. These men are making profitable business deals while the hot wind blows and the sun scorches everything in sight.

My friends and I step out of the bus and gather around our guide. He tells us, "Allah gave the donkey first and the camel second." I silently wonder, What is that supposed to mean? Our guide is so sure of himself, I am certain he will not be able to fathom that I cannot fathom what he means. So, I do not ask him to explain, and I remain silent.

As we stand in a blazing 125 degrees Fahrenheit, we are buffeted by winds blasting us with thousands of gritty sand particles. Our guide continues, "Four prices for the camel. One, you give price. Two, you pay cash now one-half and one-half later; five hundred or six hundred apiece. Three, agent goes to owner and agrees. Price is one million for each camel." I don't know what step four is; our guide doesn't tell us. Maybe it is implicit that it is the final sale. Or maybe I am so distracted by how hot I am, and how much sand is sticking to my sweaty skin, that I didn't hear him say what it was.

Our guide carries on, "There are trucks full of alfalfa to eat and some grain. Lose five camels out of one-hundred on the way here from Western Sudan where it's green. Trees with thorns, that's why upper lip is heart-shaped, parted, for eating acacia trees."

I'm sweating profusely, and not feeling what you'd call comfortable. My moist hand is sticking to my writing tablet, but I'm determined to continue to take notes on the information our guide is giving to us. He continues, "Much baksheesh in Egypt. Here, in Sudan, as you know, they cooperate totally." I understand what he is saying; baksheesh, in this case, means bribe money. So, he is saying that in Egypt they use a lot of bribe money, but bribe money is not necessary in Sudan. I believe he is telling us the truth.

Our guide then says, deliberately and firmly, "Each camel has feelings and a personality."

As the hot wind whips through the camel market I think, This is typical for Sudan. A hot wind always blows. It feels as if someone opened a door to a blast furnace, and I'm standing directly in front of that furnace right now. And yet, I never see tempers rise in Sudan. Incredible!

Hordes of black flies swarm around us, everywhere, including flies in the dirt in which we are walking.

I see many handsome, brown-colored faces under stark-white turbans.

Out of nowhere, our guide points to a man close by, and he asks, "Do you find it odd that there is a traveling perfume salesman over there?"

He then looks directly at me. I look back at him, and smile slightly while shrugging my shoulders. I haven't the slightest idea if it's normal for a travelling perfume salesman to be at the camel market, or not.

Without answering the question he just asked, our guide herds our group onward.

With this mystery on my mind and a growing smile on my face, I bring to a close my close encounters with camels, those ill-tempered, endearing, complex creatures of desert endurance.

Chapter 12

COED BATHROOM PARADOX

The swimming pool at the Hilton Hotel is cleared of all women every day at 5 p.m. so the Muslim men can swim in it. In this culture men and women do not mix in public, and this definitely includes women in swimming suits. But, the other night I walked into the women's bathroom at the Hilton and a man was cleaning the toilets and the counters. While he was accomplishing his cleaning responsibilities, there were several Sudanese women in that same bathroom. Those women were going to the bathroom in individual stalls and paying no attention whatsoever to the man who was cleaning the toilets in the stalls right next to them. They also paid no attention to him as he was cleaning the counter where they were standing and smoothing their polyester dresses, or as he was washing the mirrors they were looking into while they took off their headscarves and fixed their hair. But, they wouldn't think of swimming in the same pool with men.

In my culture, a man would never be allowed to clean a bathroom when women are present in that bathroom, but men and women swim together in the same swimming pool without thinking twice about it. In this culture men and women are separated on almost every occasion, including meal time, but a man can be cleaning a bathroom where women are taking care of their personal business. Every culture has its inconsistencies, and every culture is usually oblivious to those inconsistencies as evidenced by the man in the bathroom full of women.

Chapter 13

CONTRABAND BEER AND SCOTTISH DANCING

Expatriates are heading for home right and left, and the expat community in Khartoum is diminishing daily due to strained relationships between the Sudanese government and nearly all the respective governments of the expatriates. My Scottish dancing buddies and I made the best of a disappointing Wednesday evening when I hosted dance practice on my deck and only six people showed up. Since we need eight people to do our dances, one of the guys made a run to Pizza Hot--that is not a misspelling--and we sat around eating pizza, laughing, talking, and drinking contraband beer.

Beer is a prize commodity in Sudan. This is a dry country, and any type of alcoholic beverage is illegal. No one can possess alcohol except for ambassadors and high-ranking embassy personnel who are legally allowed to possess any type of alcohol. I bought my contraband beer from a teacher who was selling it because he was leaving Khartoum; he had purchased it from an ambassador. Each time that beer changed hands the price went up. I paid about $4.00 per beer for a total of twenty beers, and it's not very good beer. It tastes watery. (I guess I've been spoiled by Pacific Northwest micro brews.) Since I am not an ambassador I am not legally allowed to have beer in my possession, but since I am not Sudanese the police won't bother me. However, if Sudanese citizens were caught by the police drinking beer in my home they could, I've been told, be taken onto the street and given forty lashes with a bullwhip.

In any case, I have very little beer and soon it will be consumed. I'm not intending to buy more because it's too expensive and, most important, I don't like the feeling of harboring an illegal substance inside my home. I wouldn't have done well concealing alcohol during Prohibition in the United States, and I don't do well here. Feeling like I have to look over my shoulder gives me the heebie-jeebies.

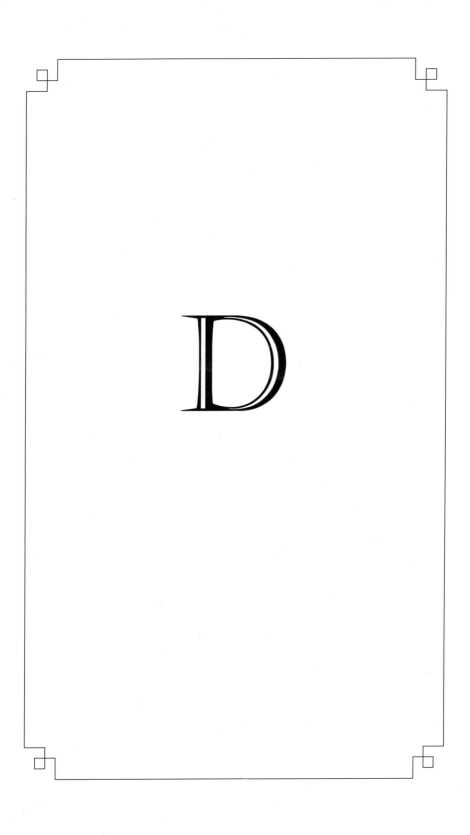

D

Chapter 14

DANCING WITH
MUSLIM WILD WOMEN

Navigating through a nasty sand storm added to the indigenous spice of my evening of dancing with Muslim Sudanese women who took off their headscarves and boogied to the beat of a gypsy drummer.

A haboob was brewing when Mustafa, the uncle of my dear friend Fatima, arrived for me in his Land Rover. His job was to drive me to the family compound in Omdurman, the oldest section of Khartoum, where there was a girls-only going-away party for Fatima and me. Fatima was returning, after a three-month visit in Sudan, to Europe and I was returning to the States for my summer vacation in Seattle.

I wanted to go to the party, but I was apprehensive about being driven in a car through a haboob. The sky was an ominous yellow, visibility was low, and the wind was high. I felt as if I were setting out into a treacherous blizzard. I voiced my apprehensions to Fatima's uncle, but he assured me, in his broken English, "It only a little haboob and there nothing worry about." Mustafa hunched forward as he clenched the steering wheel. We crept along in semi-darkness; the low visibility was a result of the wildly swirling sand which almost totally obscured the daylight. That drive should have taken no more than thirty minutes, but it took us a good hour and a half as we inched our way from Khartoum to Omdurman.

Mustafa dropped me off in front of the family compound. I squinted my eyes in the wind and sand-filled air, and made my way inside the gate. From there I stumbled to the center courtyard where there were about fifty Sudanese women of all ages and a handful of children, both female and male. Adhering to Sudanese-Muslim custom, boys up to the age of ten were allowed to attend this women's-only event. All the women were relatives or neighbors of Fatima and her family. When I arrived they were sitting in chairs and talking in loud and animated conversations, drinking fruit drinks, laughing heartily, and eating, and eating, and eating sweets. I thought to myself, No wonder these Sudanese women are hefty. They have no compunction about eating lots of food and enjoying every morsel without feeling guilty.

Then the music began. It was played by a solitary woman who beat on a brown drum made of animal skin which she tucked under her left arm. This musician had been hired to play for this evening's party by Fatima's aunts. She was a dark-complexioned, stereotypical gypsy-looking woman. She sang her songs as if by incantation, with an abandon which resides only in those who have had no formal music training, and in whom music lives so deeply that it oozes from the depths of their souls and stirs the other members of the tribe, such as me for that evening, to dance to the rhythm of her gift with a freedom I had never before felt.

All of the women were unabashedly headscarf free as they danced, and danced, and danced. They shook, rattled, and rolled their bodies all night long. During the evening some of the women hunkered in, close to my body and face, and explained, "We can really let loose and dance tonight because there aren't any men around."

At times they were dancing in their own, individual worlds without any concern for what any other woman was doing with her body. At other times they formed a large, uproarious circle in which they would place one woman in the center. With everyone's attention focused on the one in the center of the circle, all the others clapped, cheered, and egged her on to dance more and more suggestively which, I am telling you, she did with fervor. When I was placed in the center, I cut loose with a wild shimmy for which they expressed their appreciation with hoots and hollers, applause and smiles, and after which they all assured me, "You are a good dancer!" After a short pause they added, "For a foreigner."

At midnight the party was going strong. All of us, including the children, had our hands on each other's waists, and were dancing in a long snake-line around the courtyard as we wove in and out of the rooms that opened onto the courtyard. However, I had to get up at 5:30 a.m. to go to work the next day. So, Fatima's uncle was hailed. (He'd been waiting on the other side of the wall surrounding the family compound.) As I boogied my way out of the courtyard to the front gate, I waved goodbye and blew kisses to my dancing friends who waved and blew kisses in return. I opened the front gate, and walked normally to Mustafa's car. The haboob was over, visibility was normal, and I was relieved.

When Fatima's uncle dropped me off in front of my house, I told him, "Shukrun jazeelen," which means, Thank you very much.

Feeling frisky from the merriment at the party, I galloped up the three flights of stairs to my apartment, opened the front door, sashayed through my living room and bedroom, and entered the bathroom. Much to my horror, a disheveled and wild-looking, mangy character was staring at me. Its skin was pockmarked with large, brown, blemishes and its hair was standing on end. My heart thumped like mad. As I gasped and recoiled in shock I wondered, How did this scruffy, mad-eyed creature manage to get past the gate guards and into my locked apartment?!

In the next instant I realized the mangy character was me. I was staring at my reflection in the bathroom mirror, and I looked scared out of my wits. I burst into a convulsion of laughter, and I understood what happened. I had been dancing in the outdoor courtyard during the haboob. The strong wind, blown by the haboob, had set my hair on end and desert sand had been deposited over my entire, sweaty body. My brand-new Hard Rock Café Cairo T-shirt (which I'd bought in a Seattle thrift store) as well as my arms and face were smeared with unsightly brown blotches.

This phenomenon had happened to all of us during the party. But, all of the other women and kids had dark-colored skin. The brown color of the desert paste blended with their skin, and their wiry hair had stayed in place, unlike mine. Your guess is as good as mine regarding why no one said anything to me about my changed appearance during the course of the evening. I'm guessing it's because my look merged with the spirit of abandonment at the party. I, indeed, looked the part of a bona fide wild woman.

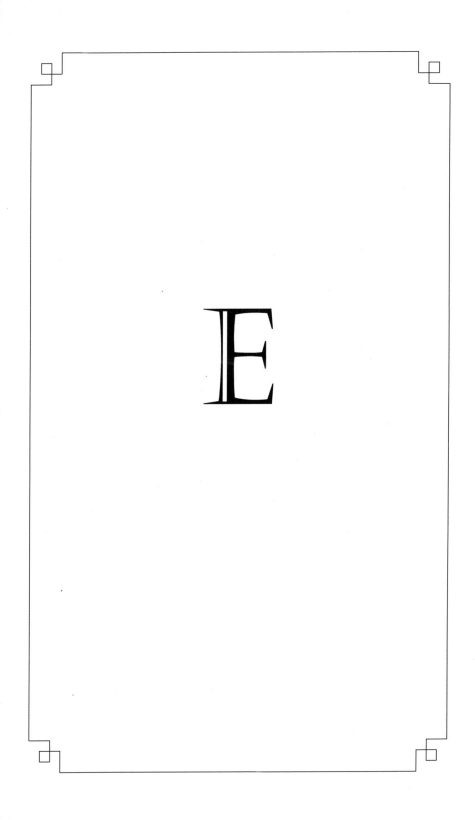

E

Chapter 15

EATING ON BEDS

When I eat a meal in a Sudanese home I usually find myself eating in the traditional Sudanese style. The fingers of my right hand are used to pluck a small piece of white bread off of a traditional, larger piece of bread (which is more or less the color, shape and size of our hot dog buns). My right-hand fingers are then cupped together, around the little piece of bread, to make a scoop which is dipped into communal bowls and plates of food. The food is supposed to be balanced on the end of the bread. It's important to be careful not to touch the shared food with any fingers, and not to touch the fingers to any part of the mouth. (I presume because fingers can be germy.) Try as I might, and I've tried very hard to master this eating technique, I'm not very good at it. My food frequently falls off my small piece of bread and splats on the table, and my fingers make contact with my mouth all too often. Fortunately the Sudanese are forgiving people.

All the while, I am seated and scrunched next to women on single beds in a bedroom. Men and women eat in separate rooms; so I'm always cozied up with women only. Their bodies are always soft, relaxed, and completely unselfconscious as they lean against my body.

Everybody uses beds in Khartoum like we use couches at home. I think that's because extended families live together, cousins frequently sleep over at each other's houses, and they all need enough beds to sleep on. Also, my guess is that there isn't enough extra square footage in most of their houses, or enough extra money, to buy beds in addition to sofas and chairs. Money is spent on beds because they are multipurpose.

Eating on beds, as well as sitting close enough to touch the other women, is foreign to my upbringing. I grew up in a house where no one hugged, or stood, or sat close enough to touch each other. Not touching was considered respectful and a sign of proper upbringing. Now I believe it is healthier to live in a manner that is respectful to one's basic nature. Living closer physically feels natural to me now. We are social creatures and appropriate touching keeps us connected at a level that words can't reach.

Chapter 16

EID CELEBRATIONS

Since men and women eat in separate rooms in Sudan, I was eating a meal on the first day of the Eid with all women. We ate in a bedroom in a humble, adobe-like house owned by my friend Ashraf's uncle. The extended family had shown respect and cultural sensitivity by giving me the one-and-only chair in the house to sit on; everyone else ate while sitting on beds. We consumed our food in the traditional, everyday way, out of communal bowls, scooping up the food with our right hands. Inside the house the turquoise-blue paint on the walls was chipping and peeling. The house had a thin, tin roof and no running water. Inside this modest home I felt fully accepted and enfolded in the family's circle of love.

The most important and traditional food was freshly barbequed lamb that had been slaughtered in the backyard while a verse of the Koran was read out loud. All of the parts of the lamb were eaten. However, Ashraf's father pointed to one of the entrées which was a dark-brown color and had a mushy consistency, and he warned me not to eat it because, "It is from a part of the sheep which will be too strange for your system to digest and not palatable for your tongue." I appreciated, respected, and abided by his protective warning.

None of the women in that household spoke any English; so, Ashraf's father, about every ten minutes or so, walked to the doorway of the bedroom where all of the women were eating. He talked to me in English to make me feel comfortable and at home. For my part, and to make the women feel at home with me, I spoke in Arabic using every word and phrase I knew. For example, I commented on the food and I told them how good it tasted, which it did, and I asked them their names. I told them where I worked and what country I was from, which I said with an attitude of jest because they all knew where I was from. They knew I was trying to make conversation with my rudimentary Arabic. This accomplished my purpose because it made them all chuckle, and relax with me.

The next day I ate with the family of another friend. The meal, including traditional lamb, was served in the formal living room of a huge house. Obvious forethought had been given to make me feel at home. My place at the table had been set with one plate and one, large, serving spoon with which to eat my entire meal. This was to excuse me from eating from the communal bowls and plates. My individual plate and spoon were, of course, familiar to me, but the house's exterior and interior were odd to me. For example, the second, third, and fourth floors remained unfinished and devoid of almost all interior walls; there were no walls on the outside of those stories of the house, and thus only the first floor was habitable. I was told that most likely the second through fourth floors always would be uninhabitable. Why uninhabitable? I don't know why (and I have seen many such houses in Khartoum).

The formal living room was constructed without any windows, which is strange to me, but common in Khartoum. This is a protection against the hot sun. The living room was decorated with bright-blue, six-foot-tall, plastic plumes sticking out of gigantic, black, plastic vases along with extra-large, paper, sweet peas made of real-life sweet pea colors. The oversized wooden chairs and coffee table were covered in brown velour with a bizarre paisley design. I tried not to stare. To me, the decor was hideous, but I reminded myself that I was in a culture completely different from my own. Had I been brought up on plumes and plastic I'd probably like it a heck of a lot better than the family-heirloom décor combined with professionally hired, classic, interior-decorator furnishings with which I was brought up, and which would most likely seem boring as all get out to these Sudanese women.

The hospitality and kindness extended to me during the Eid would be similar to us, in the U. S., inviting a Muslim to share Christmas celebrations with our families and friends. I felt deeply honored to be included in the holy Eid meals in a variety of homes all brimming with love for Allah, love for each other, and love for me.

Chapter 17

ESSENTIALS: TOILET PAPER, MONEY AND WATER

I carry a bundle of toilet paper, wads of currency, and containers of boiled water everywhere I go in Khartoum.

You have to bring your own TP because you can't buy it in any of the stores. It's not made here, and it's not imported. I brought all of mine with me from Seattle. One of my job perks was 500 kilos of my personal possessions shipped from Seattle to Khartoum, paid in full by my school. In my allotted kilos I included enough toilet paper to take me comfortably through two years in Khartoum. You might wonder how I knew how much to bring. To determine that amount, I counted how many rolls I used in two weeks in Seattle and I multiplied that by the number of weeks I would be living in Khartoum. I also added several extra rolls for anticipated bouts with dysentery. So far, so good; my calculations are perfect.

As for money, no businesses accept charge cards in Khartoum. All transactions are paid in full in cash and, because inflation is rampant, two gigantic fistfuls of the largest denomination of Sudanese bills is equal to about $10.00 in U.S. currency. It is not uncommon to see people on the streets of Khartoum carrying multiple, plastic, grocery bags stuffed with bills. I stow my money inside my durable, gray backpack.

As for water, drinking tap water assures exposure to disease and quite possibly death for someone with a Western gut like mine, and there isn't any bottled water anywhere. I can't drink any of the local water unless it has been boiled for a minimum of twenty minutes to kill all of the germs that my gut can't tolerate. Before I begin to boil the water on my electric stove, my non air conditioned kitchen is already at least 100 degrees Fahrenheit. So, by the time I've finished boiling water, my kitchen is at least 110 degrees and I'm soaked with sweat. And there's more. Before I boil the water I have to filter the water, and after I boil the water I have to cool it which is not easy to do in 110 degrees, and then I have to place it in containers for consumption. Thus, water has become a major preoccupation because I have to filter it, boil it, cool it, store it, and then remember to bring it with me whenever I leave my apartment.

A few weeks ago I decided that I was being an uptight Westerner, and boiling the local water was not necessary. The day I decided to stop boiling water, I happened to be at a brunch where I talked to an engineer from Germany whose specialty is dams. He gave me a blood-curdling report. He'd just returned from an inspection of the Domazine Dam which holds the water for Khartoum. There'd been a cholera outbreak in that area, resulting in many animals and people dying. He gave me firsthand details of dead cattle and dead people floating in the reservoir. During that conversation I decided I'll continue to boil water and sweat in my kitchen because I'd rather be hot and inconvenienced than dead.

I'll keep on stowing my water along with wads of money and toilet paper inside my trusty backpack wherever I go, without complaining.

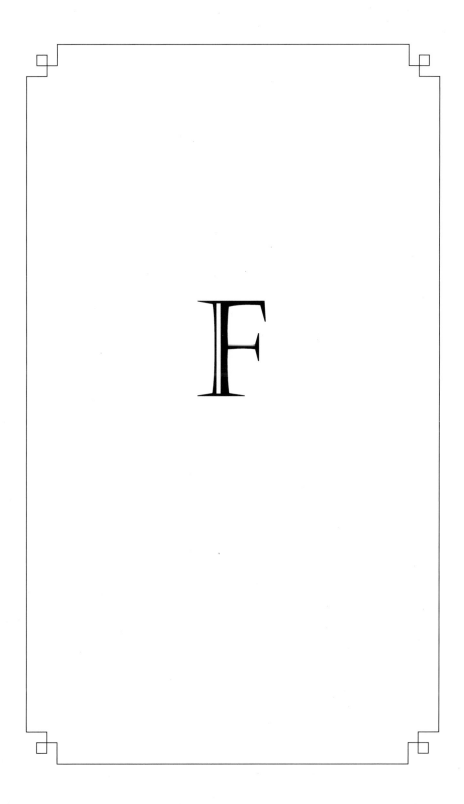

Chapter 18

FAMILY

After being in transit for thirty-six houis from Seattle to Khartoum, I felt assaulted by an August 9th temperature of 125 degrees Fahrenheit. I had just spent a glorious summer vacation with friends in Seattle in moderate temperatures. Exhausted from the flights and layovers, I was dreading the unavoidable ordeal at Khartoum International Airport. If you, the reader, have already read the chapter titled "Airport Blues" you will understand my dread and thus my utter relief when I saw, much to my surprise, my Arabic teacher, Ashraf, and several of his family members smiling and waving to me from the other side of the customs agents. When I saw them I literally began thanking God.

Ashraf was looking very spiffy in his Western-style black jeans, black suspenders, and a T-shirt. His father and his uncles were dressed in white jalabeyas. Ashraf's mother was wearing a traditional Sudanese tobe under which she wore an A-line skirt and a simple blouse. How reassuring it was to have my Sudanese "family" welcoming me back to my home away from home.

I cleared customs after the expected brouhaha. (This time the hassle happened because they didn't want to believe that only non-alcoholic water was in my nalgene container.) Caravanning in three cars, Ashraf's family escorted me to my apartment. The men carried my bags up the three flights of stairs and into my living room. I immediately offered to unpack my bags, and give them their gifts which I'd purchased in Seattle.

Before I left Khartoum for my summer break, I asked each member of this remarkably considerate family what they wanted me to bring to them from the States. Each person was reluctant to tell me what he or she wanted for gifts. They explained to me that they had befriended and assisted me during my first year in Khartoum without any expectation of gaining anything material in return. I insisted that it was culturally appropriate for me to give back and, most important, I wanted to give to them in return because they had given so much to me. In the end, I obtained a list from each person of items that are not obtainable in Sudan, and I was pleased because all of these things were within my budget. During my summer in Seattle I did my best to fulfill each person's wishes. For example, with the help of friends, I found sixteen of the twenty videos requested by Ashraf, specific reference books for Ashraf's father, and a stuffed animal for Ashraf's sister.

Now the family deferred the gift giving, telling me that I must be very tired from my travels and I needed time to adjust to Khartoum. True to their values, they kept my interest at heart and not their own.

After I changed my clothes we left my apartment and drove to their house where we dropped off Ashraf's family. Ashraf and his friend Hassan then drove me to the Nile River. There we played guess-a-word games in English, in the sand, along the banks of the Nile River. The game went like this: one person would draw, with his or her toes, an individual space in the sand for each letter of a mystery word. The other two would then start to guess letters of the mystery word, and the one in charge of that word would draw the correctly guessed letters in the blank spaces. The challenge was to guess the mystery word when the fewest possible letters were filled in.

What gave the game a unique twist was that Ashraf and Hassan messed up, a lot, on their spelling. For example, Hassan spelled Chevrolet as Chivralet when he was in charge of the mystery word, and Ashraf spelled organization as orgunezashin. I must say that I thought highly of them for getting this close to the correct spelling. Arabic and English are entirely different from each other in their origins and structures.

After about twenty minutes of playing the game with misspellings, I knew we needed a practical, ego-protecting, meaningful, and fun way of going about the game. I said, "How about this. I'll be the one to spell the words. I'll concentrate on one letter at a time, and you can see if it's easier for you to play the game that way." In other words, I would give them the correct letters via ESP. We discovered that the game was much more enjoyable, and much easier to play when we connected and concentrated via ESP rather than on the words.

After several successfully spelled words, Ashraf said to me, "We still have our good connection!" and I agreed. Ashraf was referring to the many times he and I had previously played ESP-related games. For example, he would promise to think of me three times in the coming week and when we met for our weekly Arabic lesson I would tell him the days and times when I "got the message" that he had been thinking about me. We discovered that we were perfectly in synch almost all of the time.

Later that evening I stood alone on the deck of my apartment gazing at the night sky, and thinking about the fact that, as we become increasingly more aware of our interconnectedness, the concept of family can extend beyond the traditional boundaries of birth, country, and religion. Real family includes those we relate to and care about in a deep and meaningful way, with whom we learn from our mistakes and cherish the good times. On my first evening back in Sudan I felt very fortunate to have a true family of the heart in Khartoum.

Chapter 19

FORTUNE TELLER MISFORTUNE

Today was the final day of Sudan Week, an annual tradition at our school, during which the students and staff experience traditional Sudanese culture. This week the school was more like a school ought to be: interesting, informative, and fun, with a myriad of interactive and hands-on activities.

This morning I rode a camel around the school grounds in a cloud of brownish-red, desert dust mixed with white, barbeque smoke. I dismounted and joined my eight sixth-grade students who were sitting contentedly in bright-orange, fiberglass, classroom chairs under the shade of the bamboo roof in our school's center courtyard. We watched traditional, Sudanese food being prepared and cooked by two of the oldest and most wrinkled Sudanese men you could ever imagine, both of whom had very dark, blue-black skin. (I had never seen this color of skin before coming to Sudan.) They each wore a traditional jalabeya and had white turbans wrapped around their heads.

Over an outdoor fire, these two men poured batter into a frying pan and cooked the mixture into a thin, white, spongy, pancake-looking thing over which they spooned a mixture of yogurt, feta cheese, and a reddish-colored, goopy sauce made from ground-up meat which had been dried, ground into a powder, seasoned with exotic spices, and then cooked. My students and I ate the pancake in the traditional Sudanese way, using the fingers of our right hands as scoops. For dessert we had the Sudanese equivalent of doughnuts. They were similar to U.S. doughnuts, but these didn't have a hole in the middle, and each one was rolled in granulated sugar after it had been deep-fried. For drinks we had cold karkaday tea and hot, thick, Turkish coffee flavored with cardamom. The food was good. I liked all of it, a lot.

Next, I waited in line for a half hour to have my fortune told by a brown-skinned, Sudanese beauty. She was draped in a bright-yellow, traditional tobe. Her black hair was braided from her forehead to the nape of her neck in alternating wide braids and skinny braids. In her closed palm she shook seven cowry shells, cast them on a table, looked at me, and said in Arabic through a translator, "What are you worrying about? After all you've been through, don't you believe that you are finally going to be happy? You are going to be very happy soon."

The fortune teller then told me that I would, "receive wonderful news soon, in a letter." She also said that I had refused many offers for marriage (she was right about that) but the next offer would be the right one, and I should marry a man at home named Jimmy who was missing me very much. Jimmy would buy me a new car, and he and I would have two children. To that I thought, Hmmm I don't know anyone named Jimmy, and I've never aspired to the scenario of a new car and two kids.

Then she told me the real kicker, "You are going to receive a lot of money soon and you have to promise me you will give me a large portion of the money when you receive it." I'm telling you, she was downright adamant about getting that promise from me. In fact she was so unwavering, my suspicions were aroused, and during that day I asked everyone who had their fortunes read by her if she had told them that they were going to receive a lot of money soon. I discovered that she had, indeed, told every person this same thing along with making them promise that they would give her a large portion of the money when they received it.

Now I ask you, the reader, why is it that there are the archetypical rip-off fortune tellers in every culture? Do you suppose it's because there are suckers in every culture? I think that fortune tellers may single-handedly be the ones to prove P.T. Barnum was right when he said, "There's a sucker born every minute."

Oh well, what the heck, it only cost 2,000 Sudanese dinars to have her read my fortune. That's roughly equivalent to U. S. $2.10 and amounts to an inexpensive reminder to not be a sucker, and to beware of fortune tellers.

Chapter 20

FRIDAY IS SUNDAY AND SUNDAY IS MONDAY

Since this is a Muslim country, Friday is equivalent to our Sabbath Sunday and thus my workweek is Sunday through Thursday which wreaks havoc inside my American-trained brain. The days of the week in Khartoum don't compute in my consciousness as they should. When someone makes a date to meet me on Monday evening it computes in my brain as the first work day of the week; so, I'm ready to go on Sunday, but actually Monday here is our Tuesday in the States. This has been befuddling. When I learned the days of the week as a young child I remember being very proud of myself; little did I know that I would need to temporarily unlearn and relearn them as an adult. This is taking some getting used to, and I'm not so sure I will ever be able to completely reprogram my mind to adjust to this.

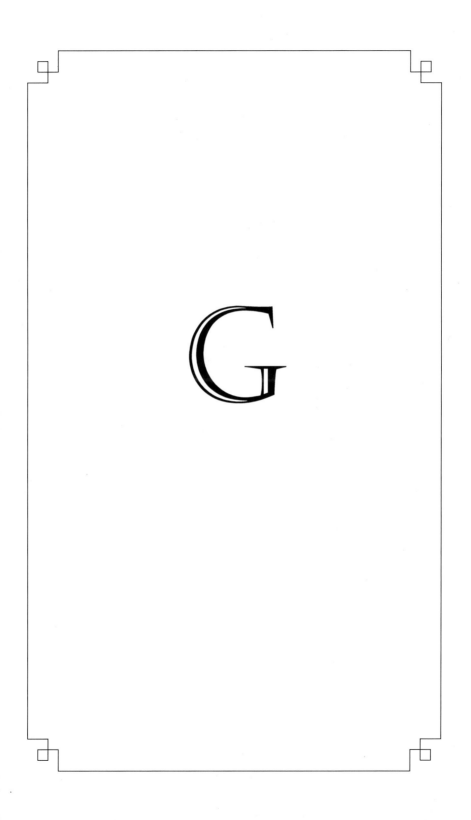

Chapter 21

GATE GUARDS

Since I refer to gate guards throughout this book I want to clarify the gate guard image. They have no guns, no knives, and no weapons of any kind. They are all peaceful, relaxed guys, just like all the men I've encountered here.

They are stationed at entrances to schools, places of business, and houses where the owners can afford them. All the houses here are cement, and all are surrounded by metal or cement walls which are approximately fifteen feet tall. Many houses and buildings have entrance gates, mine included, made of wrought iron which is fashioned into art deco-ish designs. The gate guards sit or stand just outside these gates, or just outside the front doors.

Other defining characteristics of the guards are: they are always male, and they almost all dress in traditional, white, cotton jalabeyas, although some dress in Western clothes such as T-shirts and comfortable pants.

I'm glad the gate guards are around because they peacefully shoo away scruffy, starved, stray animals and potentially bothersome beggars.

Chapter 22

GAY

Yes, Sudan is a Muslim country and yes, there are gay men in Khartoum. How do I know? I'll tell you.

One evening I was invited to an extravagant birthday party in Khartoum at the luxurious home of a European acquaintance of mine. He has worked as a respected professional in the Arab world for many years. His large home was brimming with a tasteful combination of Arab and Western furnishings.

I was one of five European-looking women at the party, and approximately one-hundred men all of whom appeared to be Sudanese. They were dressed in starched, white, traditional jalabeyas. Based on the flirtatious behavior of the men at the party, all of them were gay including the host, which was a big surprise to me. Now I know for sure that gay men do exist in the Muslim world. They gather together despite the threat of serious repercussions and because these repercussions are real, I intentionally gave no details here.

Chapter 23

GHOST STORY

The beleaguered, run-down bus transporting the Sudan Archeological Society's field trip participants chugged into Khartoum after dark. The incessant desert wind had whipped sand into every exposed orifice of my body. As soon as I was back in my apartment I took an extra-long shower, tucked myself into bed, and promptly fell asleep.

In the wee hours of the morning, I had a short-lived but terrifying experience. I was visited by a dead man whose grave I'd robbed earlier in the day. Yes, it's true and I'm not proud of it. I, along with several other member of the Archeological Society, robbed his grave.

I'll explain.

We'd gone on an all-day excursion. Before boarding the bus for our return trip to Khartoum, a handful of us roamed the desert together for a half hour, or so, and we came upon a fresh gravesite. Placed on top of a mound of sand were many exotic items, and under the mound was presumably the body of the deceased. A grave-robbing frenzy commenced as Archeological Society members swarmed around, and on top of, the mound. I stood still, watching, aghast as one person snatched a really cool lantern, and others plucked enticing, hand-tooled items.

I argued back and forth in my mind, saying to myself, Should I? No! I shouldn't! Yes, I should! No, I shouldn't!

After a few minutes of internal arguing, I succumbed and dashed to the mound. I grabbed a black, rectangular-shaped piece of leather I'd been eyeing. It was about two inches by one inch, and had a handsome, intricate, hand-tooled pattern. A small voice inside my head was counseling me, saying, You know you shouldn't be doing this. But, the egocentric and grabby part of me silently whined, I want some loot, too. And the competitive part of me asserted to myself, No one else sees that lovely piece of leather. I'll claim it for mine.

Sure enough, a chorus of, "Oooohs," and, "Aaaaahs," rang out as the others spied my booty. Such a fine piece of leather work! Just then we heard our bus driver honking the horn in the distance and we all scurried across the desert sand, some smug with their newly found treasures, others disappointed. We clambered onto the bus and settled in for a long, jostling ride back to Khartoum.

That night, in the dead of the night, I awoke with a start. I knew that an intruder was in my bedroom. In the following few seconds, as I was coming into a fully-awakened state, I saw him. He stood at the door to my bedroom dressed in his traditional, white jalabeya with a dark-colored vest. He was vibrant and strong, with chocolate-colored skin, looked to be about forty-five years old, and was transparent. He stared at me intently. I knew it was the man whose grave we'd robbed.

In a split second I was fully awake, and he disappeared.

I lay wide awake for hours, alarmed and wondering what to do. It seemed that he meant no bodily harm. Nonetheless, his male, energetic presence inside my locked apartment had given me quite a scare. I suspected that his motivation was curiosity, and he had come to see where his piece of leather had ended up. That was my suspicion, but I wasn't at all sure.

I decided it was best to talk to a native Sudanese about this dicey situation. Several days later I explained the circumstances to the wisest Sudanese man I knew. I felt comfortable talking with him because his family has more or less adopted me into their family. He didn't raise an eyebrow as he listened to my story. When I finished talking, he spoke to me matter-of-factly without a hint of judgment or blame. With a kind tone in his voice, he said, "The Koran tells us about things like this. The next time he comes, if he comes again, ask him what he wants." I agreed with my friend's down-to-earth and sage advice.

The Sudanese ghost never returned. I feel thankful for yet another lesson learned in the uncompromising desert. I knew better than to let my ego lead, and it led me straight into an unforgettable and for-real nightmare. Once again, I'd been taught the importance of paying attention to, and following, the counsel of that small, knowing voice.

Chapter 24

GOD EITHER LAUGHED OR CRIED

Two motorcycle dudes were enjoying their afternoon coffee in a Khartoum restaurant where a friend of mine just happened to be having coffee, too. She struck up a conversation with these two strangers, and a few hours later she and I were riding on the backs of their motorcycles. I spent the following several days riding around Khartoum with my arms and hands wrapped around the torso of a fine specimen of a South African man named Peter. I straddled the back end of his magnificent motorcycle with an enormous smile stretched across my face. Helmetless.

As we roared and bounced through the rutted streets of Khartoum, I felt as if I was riding in a VIP motorcade. Cars screeched to a halt, and beckoned us to pass in front of them. Hundreds of Sudanese men lined up along the sides of the streets, their eyes glued on us while they smiled, waved, and hollered, "Welcome in Sudan!" or, "Hullo!"

As we drove along the bumpy, potholed streets of Khartoum, several times I was bounced clear off the seat into midair, and I loved it. What a wild ride.

Where do you think Sandy and I took these two hot dudes on Friday night? Of course! To Chicken Street. We paraded down Chicken Street in a cloud of brown road dust mixed with gray-white barbeque smoke. Dismounting that beast of a machine took some effort, and within seconds we were surrounded by a crowd of boys and men chattering in Arabic and pointing at the road hogs. Rather than remain a spectacle, we ordered our chicken "to go" and the proprietor wrapped it in thin, brown paper. We traveled back to my apartment on streets lined with exuberant, well-wishing spectators, and then we ate our barbequed chicken in privacy on my outdoor deck. As we enjoyed a leisurely dinner we talked about <u>Zen and the Art of Motorcycle Maintenance</u>, life in Khartoum, their travels from South Africa to Sudan, and their plan to reach London on their motorcycles within the next four months.

During dinner that evening, I learned that Gary met Peter when he answered the ad that Peter placed in a Cape Town newspaper advertising for a companion to motorcycle with him on his journey from South Africa to London, England. Peter said his wife had suddenly left him and he simultaneously lost his job, so what else was there to do but take a long adventure on a motorcycle. Since he didn't want to go it alone, he put an ad in the paper asking for a companion. Here they were, high and dry in Khartoum awaiting a replacement part for Peter's motorcycle. They couldn't go any further until the part arrived, and was successfully installed. The missing motorcycle part, by the way, was the cause for me bouncing off the seat during that wild ride.

They had been on the road for months, and had just spent several grueling weeks in Ethiopia where they were afraid their clothes would literally be torn off their bodies. Aggressive Ethiopian hands were constantly trying to snatch anything and everything from their saddle bags. Gary and Peter were suspicious that this behavior resulted from the fact that Ethiopians have received aid in the form of easy money for so long it has done them a disservice; now they have an attitude that they are entitled to handouts in any form from those who seemingly have more than they have.

Sudan, on the other hand, has received next to no aid. Gary and Peter knew when they'd crossed the border from Ethiopia into Sudan because of the difference in the demeanor of the people. They said that Sudan was the only African country with friendly people. They arrived in Sudan late in the afternoon after an arduous day of pushing their motorcycles more often than they could ride them through the searing desert sand because the sand was too deep to ride in. This had happened despite the fact that their bikes had been designed by the Brits during the colonial era specifically for riding in the Sahara Desert. They described themselves as, "hot, dead tired, and icky dirty," when they entered Sudan. They saw, way out in the distant desert, what looked like a lean-to. Several minutes later, they saw what looked like several men walking out of the lean-to toward them. When the men got to Peter and Gary, they handed each of them a Pepsi and welcomed them to Sudan. Then, they graciously took their motorcycles from them, and those kind Sudanese men pushed the bikes all the way to their lean-to. On top of all of that, those Sudanese gentlemen hardly had a cent to their names, but they wouldn't let the travelers pay for their drinks. Peter and Gary said, "We were treated like guests! How is it that the most gentle, friendly people have inherited the most hostile, ugly landscape in Africa? It's unfair."

"But," I said, "they maintain a sense of humor and an attitude of relaxed acceptance about it all. I've seen many Sudanese people smile, and then in an ever so lighthearted way, they say, 'God either laughed or cried when he made Sudan.'"

In this tough desert, the inhabitants have an abiding faith that brings a depth of understanding. Their faith goes beyond the heat and the harsh landscape, and guides them to a deep acceptance of life and for all God's creatures, including those who are icky dirty.

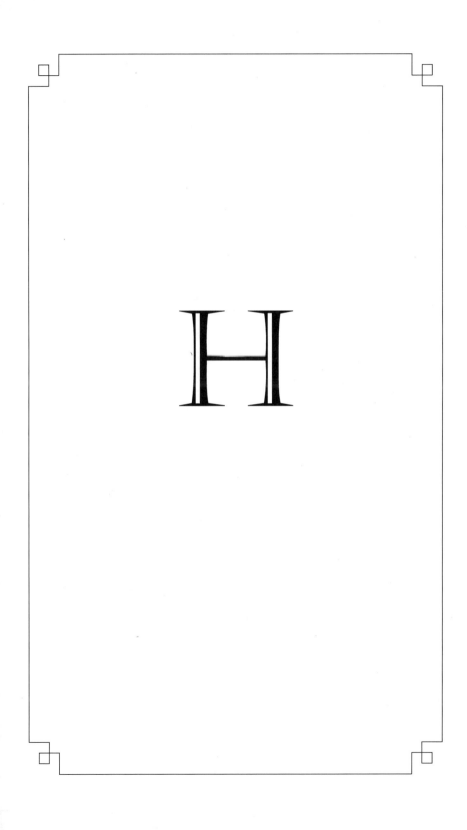

H

Chapter 25

HEAT AND HABOOBS

If you were to ask me, "How's the weather in Sudan?"

I would answer, "There are two seasons, hot and scorching hot."

If you were to ask the Sudanese, they would most likely answer, "We have two seasons, winter and summer."

The summer months prevail from April through approximately mid-November. Starting in May, our school's outdoor temperature gauge easily rose to 130 degrees Fahrenheit on most days. Such is life in one of the hottest capital cities on the planet.

When the desert starts to heat up to those unbearable temperatures, it's a seller's market for diesel generators in Khartoum. During those scorching-hot months the demand for electricity exceeds the capacity of the dam on the Nile to produce electricity. The government's solution is to cut the electricity in the various neighborhoods for several willy-nilly hours every day. If you're fortunate enough to have the money to buy a generator and the fuel to power it, you have electricity despite the daily cuts.

My house has a generator. It sounds and smells like a humungous Mac truck is idling in the front yard whenever it's switched on. I don't complain because it keeps the refrigerator humming, computer powered, water cooler whirring in the living room, shower flowing, bedroom air conditioner blasting, and the water pumping to my water taps. The generator racket jangles my nerves, but it's nice to be able to cool my house to a reasonable

85 degrees when it's 130 degrees outside, and I like having all of the electrically-powered conveniences up and running.

A personal and ongoing heat-related frustration is that my skin constantly prickles from a heat rash. Since I've never before lived in temperatures this high, I didn't know I was susceptible until I moved here. The red bumps on my midriff are a nuisance and the prickly feeling is a constant irritation. Thankfully it fades away during the cooler months.

Winter arrived on November 11th during my first year in Khartoum. How did I know? I knew because, when I got to work at 7 a.m., I noticed that the groundskeepers had taken off their white, cotton turbans and they had wrapped gray, wool mufflers around their heads. They were continuing to wear their wool headpieces when I left work at 3:15 p.m. It did not feel like wool-necessary weather to me. So, I checked the temperature gauge which hangs in the shade outside our school's main office. My suspicions were confirmed. The temperature registered 96 degrees Fahrenheit. This was absolutely not a wintertime or wool headpiece-wearing temperature to me, but it was to the workers. This illustrates the point that cultural contexts and perceptions are all relative.

When the so-called winter season arrives, the temperature drops to a tolerable, daytime range in the high 80s and mid 90s, and the troublesome haboob season ends. This is a huge relief because haboobs are nasty, wet windstorms that descend with a fury. (Haboob, by the way, is pronounced exactly like you'd expect it to be pronounced which is hu-boob, with the emphasis on boob, which makes it a strange word to the English-trained ear.) The high winds are often accompanied by thunder and lightning, and they always dump large, sloppy globs of rain which are heavy with desert sand. These giant drops plop and splat in blobs that accumulate quickly, and usually leave the city flooded for several days. Sometimes the rainblobs (I think this is a fitting, albeit made-up, word) cause power outages because they are heavy with desert sand and they weigh down everything, including power lines.

Haboobs arrive unannounced. You don't know they're speeding toward you until you see them on the horizon. I've watched them from my deck. From a distance they resemble a mile-high, yellowish-brown fog bank. As the menacing wall of desert sand approaches, I scurry around my deck carrying the outdoor furniture indoors so it won't be blown into the neighborhood.

After it subsides, everything has a thick, condensed layer of sand coating it and that includes the clothes on your body, your body itself, both the inside and outside of your vehicle, and your dwelling. I always take a shower to clean the gritty sand off of, and out of, my body. My house and deck are in need of a thorough dredging, too.

I've weathered ten haboobs.

I'll never forget the moment when I saw my first haboob during my first year in Khartoum. My friend Tommy, who had lived in Khartoum for several years and was thus a survivor of many such tempests, was jogging up the outside steps leading to my apartment for an unexpected visit. I happened to be strolling on my deck, and I was looking at what appeared to be a mile-high wall of golden-brown desert dirt rolling toward Khartoum from the southeast. I called out to him, "Hey, Tommy! Would you please hurry, and come up here, and tell me if there is a haboob approaching?" Since he was an airline pilot, I figured he knew about weather-related things. He arrived at my door, walked to the southeast side of my deck with me, stared in silence for a full minute and said, ever true to his super-polite personality, "Yes, yes, it is. It is. Excuse me. I, I, I must be going home now." He sprinted down my stairs, and down the street as if his pants were on fire. Good thing, too, because ten minutes later the storm slammed into my sturdy, cement, apartment building with such force that the building shook and shuddered. The desert sand blew into my eyes and they felt as if they were being scraped with sandpaper. I dashed inside to take shelter.

In case you were wondering about Tommy, I spoke with him a few days later. He told me that he had reached his apartment, tucked himself safely inside, and seconds later the haboob hit.

One haboob that was particularly memorable snuck up on me in the middle of the night. I'd fallen asleep on my living room couch, and I awakened to the sound of the fronds of giant palm trees, two blocks away, being tossed back and forth violently by the storm. I jumped off of the couch and onto my cement floor, pulled on an ankle-length, African, tie-dyed housedress over my naked body, crammed my feet into my running shoes, and dashed onto my patio to rescue my purple, red, and yellow windsock which I had hand-carried all the way from Seattle. It was a summer birthday present given to me by two dear friends, and had sentimental value. My dress billowed and flapped wildly as the wind yanked on the windsock which was hanging from the rafters of the roof that covered a portion of my patio. After several unsuccessful attempts, I wrestled my windsock to safety, but not before plump globs of wet desert sand were dumped all over me.

Another particularly bad haboob arrived at a decidedly inopportune time for our school. It struck when all of our school's teachers were setting out for Nairobi where we were scheduled to attend the annual East African Teachers' Conference. The driver from our school picked me up, as had been prearranged, at 12:45 a.m. and the storm was in full swing. As we pulled away from my apartment I was witnessing the most ferocious thunder and lightning I had ever seen in my life, and the streets of Khartoum were inundated with streams of water making for a slow and treacherous drive. There were mud puddles the size of small ponds everywhere.

During that slow drive to the airport my mind replayed the details of many stories I'd been told of people who, during haboobs, disappeared into mud puddles that actually were not puddles, but holes deep enough to swallow a car and its occupants. We didn't disappear into any potholes that night, and we did make it to the airport. However, as a result of the high winds and the flooding, our plane took off five hours later than scheduled.

All night, while Khartoum was ravaged, the other teachers and I fidgeted and squirmed in misshapen plastic chairs in the airport where there were no refreshments of any kind, no water fountain, no functioning toilet, and no toilet paper. To keep myself calm I told myself, Since you can't change it, you might as well flow with it; you accept it and go with it, or you rail against it and upset yourself about it. Looking on the upside, I felt blessed that our plane waited until conditions were safe to fly out of Khartoum.

I've been told by several local people, "You haven't seen a real haboob yet, just wait." I hope I don't see a real one. People die in real ones. One Sudanese friend told me that her father-in-law was a passenger in a plane that could not land because of low visibility. The plane circled, and circled over Khartoum, eventually running out of fuel and crash landing. Everyone on board was killed.

Haboob troubled and scorching-hot Sudan has not escaped the warming trend on the planet. Sudanese residents in my neighborhood, as well as those who are friends of mine, have told me that they know Sudan is warmer now because they no longer need to wear jackets during the winter months. They are quite comfortable wearing short-sleeved shirts and blouses all winter long. They spoke with great concern about the effects of this trend because Sudan is already uncomfortably hot, even for the locals. With more heat the temperatures would easily go beyond 130 degrees. One wonders how much heat a human being can tolerate physically and emotionally, and what will happen to the vegetation, animals, fish and reptiles when scorching hot becomes even hotter?

When I leave Sudan I won't miss the heat or the haboobs. Living here has made me feel all the more thankful that I call Seattle my home, and I swear I will never again complain about Seattle's gray skies and gentle rain. However, I will miss my good friends here, and the prevailing spirit of the Sudanese people who remain consistently friendly, relaxed, helpful, generous, respectful and thoughtful despite the challenging weather. This confirms to me that life is, indeed, a matter of attitude.

Chapter 26

HOLY HAND HOLDING

One morning during Ramadan the call to prayer blared at 2:30 a.m. from the loud speakers in the large mosque a block from my house. It had never happened that early or sounded that loud. I lay in bed for several minutes. The decibel level accomplished its purpose and made sleeping impossible. I got up, slipped into a batik caftan, and walked outside onto my deck. I looked down at the street, and what a sight to behold! Hundreds of silent men flowed towards the mosque. Dressed in white turbans with their white jalabeyas gently waving in the early morning breeze, their shoes softly crunched along the dirt road as they walked in absolute silence.

Many of the men were walking side by side and holding hands. I liked watching this holy hand holding. As I watched the men, I thought about all the countries I've lived in and visited where hand holding of same-sex people is considered to be perfectly natural. I'd like to see this custom imported to the United States for men and for women, albeit this could take some getting used to.

I remember the first time my adult hand was held by another same-sex adult and I was mighty uncomfortable, but only for the first couple of minutes. It happened years ago in Bogotá, Colombia, when an older woman who had befriended me, volunteered to take me shopping for groceries and necessities. I felt very uneasy for the first few minutes during our first day of shopping together because she held my hand firmly, and wouldn't let go for anything. In no time at all, this custom made perfect sense to me because she was matter of fact and unselfconscious about it, and I had a dependable guide and trusted companion at my side in a frightfully busy, congested, unsafe, Spanish speaking and foreign metropolis.

Now I consider adult hand holding to be a natural and unspoken extension of caring and friendship, as demonstrated by these men making their way to their mosque during the holy month of Ramadan.

Chapter 27

HONESTY

I, along with three other teachers, hoped for the best when we rented a table at the annual Khartoum American School bazaar where we displayed and sold our stuff. My stuff included things I brought with me from Seattle that I hadn't used, such as: unopened jars of Grey Poupon Mustard, hair bands, a black-and-white silk scarf, a doll dressed up in a Halloween costume, and some stinky perfume that a Seattle friend gave me for a going-away gag gift.

There were lots of vendors at the bazaar selling local crafts, but most of the shoppers were Sudanese and they wanted goods brought from, or made in, the United States. There was an eager crowd of people three-deep around my end of the table from 9:30 a.m. until 11:30 a.m. The bazaar was open until 4 p.m., but by noon I'd sold 90 percent of my wares. I bid the other teacher adieu, packed up my remaining few items, and I closed my shop.

I made the equivalent of $200.00 U.S. dollars in two-and-a-half hours and I had a great time doing it. (Hey! I got fourteen dollars for that smelly cologne. Can you believe it?) Rock and roll music blared from loud speakers, so while I was selling I was dancing and clapping my hands in time to the music. Everyone expected to bargain and I bargained my buns off, making deals left and right. I had the crowd smiling, laughing, moving to the music, and enjoying themselves while spending lots of money at my end of the table.

Now for the clincher. During the bazaar, I stuffed all the money I made into a large, tin, powdered-milk container which I kept under our table in an accessible place. I left the bazaar carrying my 400,000 Sudanese dinars in a black, plastic sack, and I walked home safely via a route that took thirty minute of fast walking. It went without question that the money would not be touched or bothered in any way, at any time, either while I was selling or while I was walking home. And 400,000 Sudanese dinars is what an average Sudanese wage earner makes in a year of work.

Imagine living in a world where all of us coexist with this much integrity and honesty on a daily basis. Based on my experience in Khartoum I know it is possible. We each simply need to do our part to make it happen.

Chapter 28

HONEY-SEEKING BEARS AND A GUARDIAN ANGEL

There is a Berber saying that goes like this, "The bear had nine songs and they were all about honey."

The number of men-bears swarming around my securely locked front door had finally diminished by May of my first year in Khartoum. I had been introduced to each of these suitors at various and sundry functions, but not much more than a simple introduction had been given. However, it was not difficult for them to figure out where I lived. (I was a Western white woman residing in an all-Sudanese neighborhood.) They came prowling around from seven in the morning until eleven at night. Since I wouldn't give those Sudanese men-bears the variety of honey they were hunting for, they eventually vanished, thank God.

One of them was a married man who followed me around for months, ever since he first spied me at the Saint Andrew's Society Ball. I wouldn't say he was pushy, but he was persistent. When I was going to Egypt for winter vacation he offered me the use of one of his condominiums in the heart of Cairo. When I was going to the Red Sea on spring break he offered me the use of one of his houses located on the shores of the Red Sea. I refused all of his offers. It befuddled him that I wasn't interested in any of his proposals for marriage, especially because he was very wealthy even by standards of wealth in the United States. It baffled him that monetary affluence wasn't a big selling point for me, and never has been. For starters, compatibly, mutual respect, and being the only wife are at the top of my list.

Our gate guards, who are employed to keep the riffraff away from our doors as well as the occasional robbers, stray dogs, and the constant beggars, always let those men inside the front gate because they drove expensive cars, usually Mercedes, and were dentists, prosperous businessmen, doctors, or worked for one of the embassies, and usually wore suits and ties. Once they were inside the front gate, they simply needed to climb the outside stairs to my third-floor apartment, and knock on my locked front gate.

However, our gate guards always refused entry to my good friend and Arabic teacher, Ashraf, even though he always arrived with one or more family members, or one or more friends, to serve as designated escorts. They arrived in beat-up cars because they were young, college students living on lean budgets. Never mind the fact that these guys were the purest and most spiritual of all of my visitors, and were always respectful both to me and my apartment.

Before Ashraf began each of my Arabic lessons, he and his escort, or escorts, usually knelt in prayer on my living room floor. While they prayed I sat still, peacefully meditating on my couch. One of the reasons I meditate is because I believe that in discipline there is freedom. Beginning each Arabic lesson with the discipline of meditation, I was clear-headed and focused, and my mind thus had the freedom to absorb as much as possible.

During our lesson I sat on a couch. Ashraf and his escort sat opposite me on a different couch, on the other side of my coffee table. How much more innocent can you get than that? Still, the gate guards always trudged up the stairs to my third-floor apartment, knocked on my front door, and asked for my permission before they let Ashraf inside the front gate even though I'd explained many times that Ashraf was a trusted and welcome friend.

The way in which Ashraf became my Arabic teacher was testimony to his character. Not long after I arrived in Khartoum, a friend invited me to join her on a Friday afternoon excursion along with Ashraf, Ashraf's brother, and their cousin to see the whirling dervishes. After the dervish ceremony concluded the men invited my friend and me to tea in a local restaurant. While we were sipping our tea, I asked the men if they knew of an Arabic instructor whom I could hire to teach me Arabic. Ashraf then offered to come to my house every Monday evening to give me Arabic lessons. He insisted on not taking any money from me because, as he explained, "My name, Ashraf, means 'honor' in Arabic. I want to live up to my name. It will be my honor to teach you Arabic free of charge." As I accepted his offer I thought to myself, We can all learn from the example of this young but wise eighteen-year-old.

Along with learning Arabic, I felt free to ask any question, no matter how perplexing or culturally sensitive, about Sudanese culture and life in Khartoum. For example, one evening I asked Ashraf, "Am I safe here?

As he furrowed his brow I could see that my question puzzled him, but he was quick to answer. "Yes, of course, you are safe here," he said, "you are surrounded by Muslims who live by the Koran." He went on to explain, "The holy Koran says, 'be kind to the seven neighbors in each direction.' You have seven neighbors in each direction who are watching over you. There is no reason for you to feel afraid or unsafe."

His answer was news to me, but to him it was a question that didn't need asking in the first place.

As for practical matters, Ashraf took me on countless errands. This was time-consuming because in Khartoum availability of everything is limited--from ink pens, to envelopes, to computer cords. And you never know until you arrive at a location if your sought-after item will be in stock, or not. Chances are it will not be in stock, and then you drive to the next location over bumpy roads in blistering heat hoping for the best, and preparing for the worst. Ashraf, for example, drove me around town for several hours in a search for the right cords for my computer, which was up and running thanks to Ashraf and one of his professors. Together they spent hours at my house installing computer programs, and hooking up the necessary voltage regulator. Since we have enormous power surges here, not to mention the numerous times every day the electricity shuts on and off unexpectedly, without a voltage regulator a computer is rendered inoperable in no time at all.

Within several months of the first of fifty, free, Monday-night Arabic lessons, I was referring to Ashraf as my malaki alharris which means guardian angel. Thus, I can attest to the fact that guardian angels can and do arrive in beat-up cars, and honey-seeking bears can and do arrive in Mercedes; and you can't count on one's level of formal education and degree of enlightenment going hand in hand. However, the gate guards didn't seem to understand any of this. Do you think this situation would have been different if colonization hadn't brought the notion that possessions and position speak louder than purity of intention? I know my answer to this question.

Chapter 29

HOOCH

Directly across the street from my house a traditional-looking Muslim man runs a tiny, innocuous-looking shop. He always wears a conventional, white jalabeya along with a conventional, white cap. Both he and the shop look innocent enough, but only at first glance.

He opens his shop doors in the late afternoon and remains open late into the night. From the nearly empty shelves inside his shop, he sells a few bottles of Pepsi, a few cans of Pif Paf (used for exterminating insects) and a small amount of baklava. Quite a combination. Since I live across the street I have an unobstructed view from my deck. Every night I observed a steady stream of men hovering around his shop accompanied by a constant exchange of money. I became curious and I began watching more closely. The more I watched, the more I saw.

The shop proprietor walks over to the neighborhood prostitute's house early each morning, unlocks her gate with a key, and lets himself inside. (How, you might ask, do I know she's a prostitute? She doesn't always close her curtains. That's how I know.) So, this shopkeeper seems to be keeping the shop of the neighborhood prostitute, in other words he seems to be her pimp. But, that's not all he pimps. I've observed him taking different men, one at a time, into the room in the back of his shop late at night. Then, I've seen the same gentleman leaving the shop early the following morning. Therefore, it seems likely that he is selling the prostitute's body to men as well as his body to men. But, that's not all he's selling.

He also sells plastic pitchers filled with a liquid which he stores in his two mini-sized refrigerators. I asked my Sudanese friends if he sells contraband liquor--all alcohol is illegal in this Muslim country just as it was during Prohibition in the United States--and my friends confirmed that he sells homemade alcohol out of his shop. When the days are hot the proprietor wears a well-practiced come-and-get-it expression on his face as he lounges seductively on top of the lift-top refrigerators from which he sells the hooch.

Thus, Khartoum is not completely dry or pious. In this regard it is comparable to all other cities in the world where there is a cross section of inhabitants making daily choices to take lower, or higher, avenues of consciousness and ways of living.

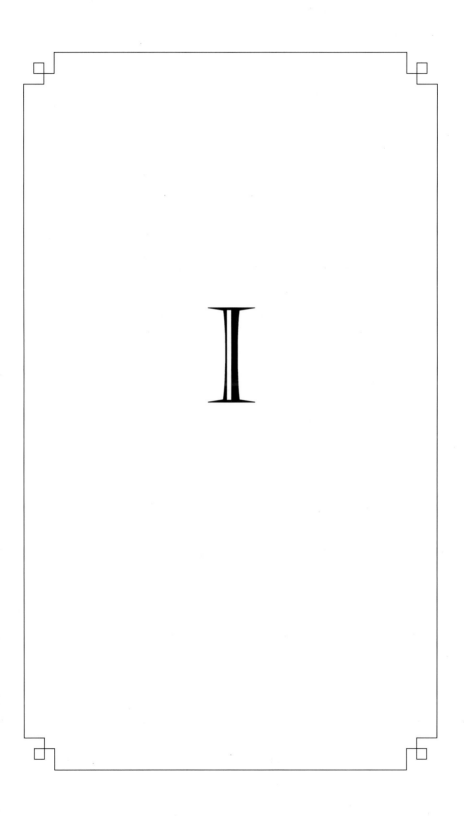

I

Chapter 30

ILLEGAL MONEY AND MONEY CHANGERS

On Halloween night during my second year in Khartoum, as I was walking to an American friend's house to see Alfred Hitchcock's film *Psycho*, I stopped at a corner grocery store in my neighborhood to make an illicit exchange of money. This was the first time for me to make an illegal money exchange in Sudan. I was a little nervous. I'd been assured by the other U.S. teachers, "That's where you do it." But, I approached this transaction with trepidation even though the store where I was to "do it" looks like any other neighborhood, Mom and Pop corner store. However, since no women are ever in evidence in any of these shops, other than as customers, I suppose one should refer to them simply as Pop stores.

These stores are numerous in Khartoum. Usually they are the size of a small kitchen in an average home in the United States. They have dirt floors, no windows, and a seven-foot by five-foot, lime-green metal door. I don't know why all of the store doors are metal and lime-green here, but they are. When the store is closed for the afternoon snooze, or for the night, those doors are locked with a large padlock placed in the center. The door is always split in two, down the middle, and one-half of the door swings open to the left and the other half swings open to the right. From these stores one can purchase all the essentials including Pepsi, Coke, and various and assorted others items such as Laundromat-sized, dinky boxes of Tide, English tea biscuits, bars of soap, matches, and fresh feta cheese.

What set this particular, hole-in-the-wall store apart from the others in my neighborhood is that the aging, Muslim proprietor runs an illegal operation inside it, exchanging U.S. one-hundred-dollar bills for Sudanese dinars. I had promised myself not to do business with this guy for the simple reason that it is illegal to change money in his store. I do not want to perpetuate illegal activities of any kind under any circumstances even though, in this instance, it was to my advantage to have him change my money because he gives a higher rate than the two legal options: local Sudanese banks, or D.H.L. (the world-wide courier service). I'd always changed my U.S. dollars to Sudanese dinars through my school, legitimately. Our school avoided cashing the teachers' U.S. checks at the banks because there is always a line with a three-hour minimum wait time. To circumvent this time-consuming process, our school ombudsman took our checks to D.H.L. where he cashed them in a matter of a few minutes, and returned to school with the appropriate amount of Sudanese dinars for each teacher.

About two weeks ago, the Khartoum D.H.L. employees got greedy. They cashed the teachers' checks twice, once to exchange the money for the teachers and once again for their own personal use. Now everyone is afraid to change money with D.H.L., and the U.S. teachers from our school needed to figure out another way to obtain local currency. Here's what we decided to do: since our paychecks from Khartoum American School are deposited electronically each month into our bank accounts back home in the United States, we decided to tell the school secretary, on a monthly basis, an amount of cash we each wanted to be paid. The secretary agreed to subtract that amount of cash from the amount deposited back home into our accounts, and give each teacher the requested amount in one-hundred dollar U.S. bills. Each teacher then takes those bills to a local money changer, gets them changed into Sudanese dinars, and uses that money for local purchases.

So, on Halloween I went to the guy at the corner store because he has a reputation for being "as honest as the day is long" and never cheating anyone. He's a typical Sudanese and a good Muslim. How do I know that? I know because his smile is gentle, and his eyes are full of light. He's also a good business man. He gives the best rate in town, higher than the banks and D.H.L. by several dinars per U.S. dollar.

The first four times I went to his shop, I appeared and departed under the cover of darkness, and I could not look the money-changer man in the eye. After he gave me my Sudanese dinars I'd mumble a few Arabic words of thanks to him, and I'd scoot out of his shop as fast as I could because I felt like a creep. One day I decided that I didn't any longer want to feel creepy about my illicit transactions with him. So, I strode into his shop at 2:30 p.m., looked him square in the eye, and beamed a smile while I said the Sudanese greeting, "Al salaam aleikum," and I handed him two one-hundred-dollar U.S. bills.

He responded with a smile and, "Wa aleikum el salaam," and he went about his business.

While he was counting my Sudanese dinars I, to appear as if I'd gone into the shop to make a purchase, I lifted two packages of English tea biscuits off the shelf and two, small sacks of Sudanese peanuts packaged by the local homeless ladies. I smiled as I gave the shopkeeper's son the 5,000 Sudanese dinars to pay for my few grocery items. The shopkeeper then handed me several, large, neat, rubber-banded, and pre-packaged stacks of Sudanese bills (which I counted later in the safety and seclusion of my apartment and verified that the correct amount of money had been given to me). I quickly shoved the pile of bills into a plastic sack, and then I tucked that sack into the bottom of my shopping bag, and our eyes met. In a voice full of gentleness and confidence he said, "Shukrun."

I replied confidently to his thank you, saying, "Afwan," which means, You're welcome.

As he and I smiled at each other, he asked, "You American?"

I answered in English and Arabic, "Yes. Anna meen Amrica." This translates as, I am from America.

He raised his right thumb toward the ceiling and said, "America good. America strong."

I nodded my head up and down, and said, "Yes. America is strong, but sometimes American is too strong. American needs to take lessons from Sudanese. Sudanese are kind. Do you understand my English?"

He smiled as he said, "Yes, I understand."

I continued, "Sudanese people are gentle. Kind and gentle. Sudanese have strong light in their eyes." I spoke slowly because I wanted him to understand every word I was saying. I placed my right hand on my heart as I said, "Sudanese are strong in the heart. This is the most important place to be strong. Strong in the heart."

He beamed as he said, "Shukrun," several times in a voice so soft it seemed as if he were offering a hushed prayer of thanks.

We smiled at each other as we exchanged the Sudanese goodbye, "Ma alsalaam," and I stepped onto the dusty street for my five-minute walk home in the hot afternoon sun.

I have returned to the money changer many times without trepidation. It seems that his brothers and cousins own the surrounding shops, and they keep an eye on each other. My hundred-dollar bills don't stay under his counter for more than five minutes. I've watched the guys from the surrounding shops move swiftly, yet discreetly, into and out of that little shop within minutes after I've handed the shopkeeper my bills. They have to move the money, in other words the evidence, out of there quickly to avoid being caught. Every few months we hear stories about all the money-changers in a particular neighborhood being rounded up by the police and carted off. I hope that my sweet money-changer doesn't meet his fate in a Sudanese jail.

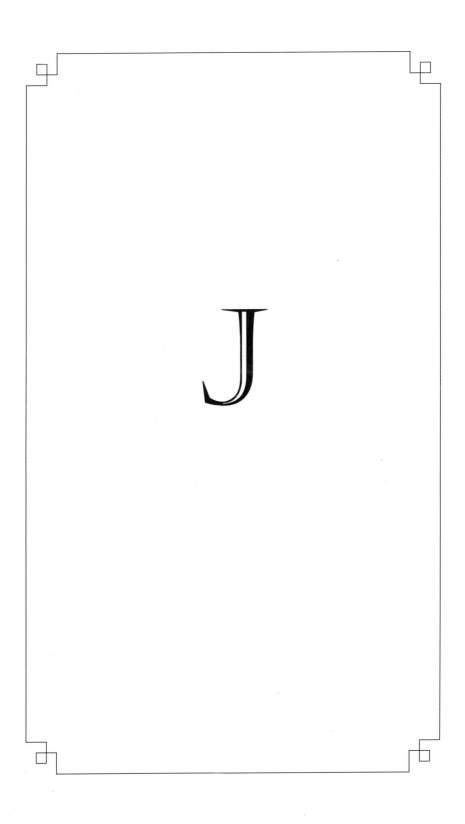

Chapter 31

JERTIK AND AN
EXOTIC, EROTIC
WEDDING DANCE

"Exotic and erotic" are the most common words used to describe Sudanese pre-wedding dance ceremonies. To say the least, that description aroused my interest, and I did my best to procure an invitation. I finally did get to attend one and I was not disappointed, not in the least.

A friend, of a friend, of a friend of mine learned that I wanted to go to a dance ceremony, and on a sizzling hot afternoon a Sudanese woman knocked on my gate at the appointed time. She did not speak English, my Arabic is minimal, and I had not previously met her. After we exchanged greetings in Arabic, I climbed into a car driven by her Arabic-speaking boyfriend who drove us to the bride's house where the ceremony was to take place.

The woman's boyfriend got out of the car, and joined the other males in a separate section of the yard where the men were to eat traditional food, drink Pepsi, and presumably talk business. It's haram, which means forbidden, for any man other than the groom to see the bride performing her wedding dances. It's also haram for anyone, including me, to take photographs of the bride and her dancing. It is believed that it will bring the bridal couple bad luck if any man, at any time, looks at any photographs of the bride-to-be doing her dances. For this reason the dances are performed in an enclosed space without windows, in this case a tent.

The Sudanese woman and I walked inside the big-top tent which had been set up outside, and beside, the bride's large house. The enormous, fully enclosed tent was made of beige canvas painted with Egyptian motifs. When I walked into the tent all eyes turned toward me. There was no hostility in their eyes, but no one seemed to expect a foreigner to be in attendance that day. My entrance seemed to take them by surprise, and I looked very different from them. I was the only European-dressed, white woman in a sea of three-hundred, traditionally dressed, brown-skinned, Sudanese women.

Imagine a dark-skinned taller-than-average African or Muslim woman dressed in her native clothes showing up unexpectedly at an all-white wedding in your home town. Don't you think you'd stop to look at her? Of course you would.

As they looked at me, I looked at them. Each woman was dressed in a traditional Sudanese tobe and high heels. Each of the three-hundred tobe fabrics was printed in a one-of-a-kind combination of dazzling colors. Added to this mix was the background of hand-painted, ancient-Egyptian motifs that covered the inside of the tent. The bright red, yellow, green, blue, and gold Egyptian themes combined with the multicolored fabrics to create an eye-popping celebration of color. Also, almost every woman was sporting freshly applied, traditional, temporary, black henna tattoos winding along her fingers and hands as well as around her feet and ankles. I thought to myself, It doesn't get any better than this for a true display of local color, and I love it!

I looked so different from them, no wonder they all looked at me. I was the only white woman, the only woman whose head was not covered, and the only woman wearing drab clothing. I was wearing a sedate, A-line, calf-length, pastel, floral-print skirt, and a moss-green, cotton top, and beige wedge heels. How boring.

Within a few minutes my entire body, including my cotton skirt and top, were drenched with sweat because the temperature in that enclosed tent must have been 130 degrees. None of the Sudanese women's tobes appeared to be sweat drenched, and that made me look all the more peculiar.

Just as quickly as their Sudanese eyes looked at me, they turned to look at the stage as the canned music started to blare and the pre-wedding dancing began. For the next forty-five minutes, I stood elbow-to-elbow in a sea of rowdy Sudanese women who were hooting, clapping, thrusting their right fists into the air in time to the music and singing along with the songs. They hollered the Arabic equivalent of, "Go girl! Shake it! Do it! Do it for your man." If you saw these women on the street you'd never guess in a million years that they were capable of such raucous behavior.

Clad in a fire-engine red, short, skin-tight dress, and a black wig of braided hair which came down to her waist, the bride-to-be danced, slithered, glided, undulated, and moved tirelessly. She wore an elaborate headdress, and wrist and ankle bracelets made of many jingling gold coins. On her hands and bare feet she was decorated with traditional black henna tattoos painted in fanciful flower designs.

Her dances looked every part professional. The series of several different dances looked like a combination of the best of erotic Egyptian belly dance, Native American powwow fancy dancing, Tahitian dancing, and dirty dancing, with a few East Indian hand mudras thrown in for good luck. She performed the dances on a raised, wooden platform in the center of a circle surrounded by the boisterous Muslim women.

The groom was either dancing with the bride or sitting next to the raised platform where she was dancing. From his seat he checked her out, boldly and suggestively from head to toe, and toe to head, again and again. He was the only male amongst a bevy of amped-up, colorful, juicy ladies.

The dancing was followed by a traditional ceremony called jertik during which the bride and groom sat in the center of the circle on a platform, and on that platform their wedding bed had been placed and adorned with a Persian rug and two satin pillows. While seated, they fed each other fresh milk from silver cups, and they spit the milk with vehemence into each other's faces while the crowd of women hooted, hollered, and roared with laughter. Since I didn't know why they did jertik, I enjoyed considering the possibilities. Maybe they were playing out their hostilities now rather than later? Or, maybe they were practicing how to express their hostilities rather than holding them inside? Your guess is as good as mine. After thinking about it, I decided that if you actually did this with your partner at home, at the least you'd end up laughing, and laughter heals many wounds. So I think jertik is worth a try.

Following the jertik, the three hundred Sudanese women guests and I sat inside the tent, eight to a circular table, and we devoured a large, Sudanese-style meal. I was seated with four women, and three young girls all of whom were from the bride's side of the family. I gleaned that information through mime gestures because none of them spoke any English.

The women at my table couldn't have been better hostesses. With large smiles and bare, sweaty hands, they reached toward the plates in the center of our table where they tore off huge hunks of grilled chicken and roasted sheep--sheep are slaughtered and then roasted over an open pit at every important occasion--and they placed the meat and poultry on my plate with gusto. With a large smile I acknowledged acceptance of their gift of food, and with my bare, sweaty hands I picked up a large chunk of sheep, stuffed it into my mouth, chewed it ravenously, and downed it. The women were thrilled with my enthusiastic display of eating, and they eagerly gave me more and more sheep and chicken. I nodded approvingly as I passionately ate more and more. In between mouthfuls I wiped, with my meat-greasy hands, sweat from my face which was pouring off me in rivulets. As the women at my table continued to beam their approval, I thought, This uptown, sit-down, bare-hands meal is as real as it gets, and the gettin' is good! I relaxed into their complete acceptance and appreciation of me and I lost all self-consciousness, and all sense of time. I was totally in synch with the real women surrounding me.

The tempo changed when my new-found friends placed different foods on my plate. All of these foods were tasty, but I could not identify by sight, smell or flavor anything I was eating except for the baba ganoush. And I began to chuckle at my sweaty, modestly-dressed self who was thoroughly enjoying every moment of this erotic, exotic, colorful and rambunctious adventure including the sight and taste of the strange foods I was eating with my bare hands.

On my way home, I wondered how my upper-crust, staid, Presbyterian mother, aunts, great aunts, and grandmothers would have reacted to that day's experiences. I know that I certainly learned a thing or two, and I'm a better woman for it.

Chapter 32

JINNS WON'T BE MENTIONED

After several days of arduous travel through the desert, our two hired vehicles, a Land Rover and a Land Cruiser, reached the glorious, turquoise Red Sea. Our first stop was a teeny island named Suakin. After crossing over a thirty-foot, two-lane, land bridge we strolled next to and through ruins of houses, mosques and buildings made of white coral which had disintegrated into shells of their former structures. Our guide told us that this port had been an important trading center for 3,000 years. It was first used as a commercial center eons ago when, in the tenth century B.C., Ramses III utilized it as a harbor for his fleet of boats which he sailed to the other side of the Red Sea with goods for trade. Our guide went on to say that the coral structures on Suakin were built in the nineteenth century during the Ottoman Empire when the slave trade flourished here. But coral requires constant upkeep and it quickly began to fall apart. As a result, in the first part of the twentieth century the center of trade was moved to Port Sudan.

Now Suakin is crumbling and abandoned. Or is it?

The name Suakin means "the inhabited land." Inhabited, you might ask, by what? The answer is: inhabited by the jinn. And what are jinn? Jinn means spirit in Arabic, and the spirits here are those of the slaves who refused to obey the commands of King Solomon, and thus the king punished them by imprisoning them on this island. The myth continues to say that the black cats on Suakin represent the jinn by day, and by night those cats become the jinn themselves.

Since we were scheduled to arrive in Port Sudan before nightfall, my five travelling companions and I had only forty-five minutes to stroll around the deserted island and catch a glimpse of, and photograph, this uniquely beautiful, crumbling, ghost town. I walked lightly on fragile Suakin that afternoon.

My recommendation to you is, "Visit this little island and experience its one-of-a-kind historic structures, but beware of black cats and take your leave before sundown."

The Sudanese will probably tell you the same thing they told me, "You don't want to mention them because you don't want to meet them."

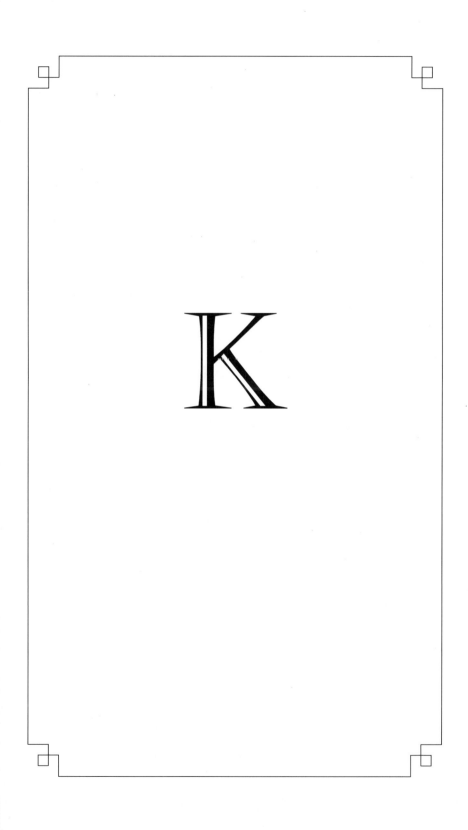

K

Chapter 33

KIDNAPPED!

A gruff, senior-ranking gate guard entered my classroom a few minutes after school was over, and barked, "You lunch appointment. You come now." That's broken English for, You have a lunch appointment. You need to come now.

I thought, He has the wrong teacher; I don't have any appointments today.

I told him, "No appointment. Me, no appointment." I always speak to the gate guards in very simple English to make sure they understand me. Their ability to both speak and understand English is limited, and my Arabic is limited. So, I always communicate with them in a mixture of simple Arabic and simple English.

The gate guard left my classroom dutifully. But, he returned in five minutes to tell me, with urgency in his voice, "Yes, you, teacher, you appointment. Lady here. Take you appointment." His urgent tone alerted me to the fact that something significant was up; but I didn't like the idea of some lady being on the premises insisting that she had a lunch appointment with me. I had not made a lunch appointment with anyone for that day.

I'd been warned to be vigilant with the Sudanese. "They always want something from you," non-Sudanese people who live here have told me repeatedly, and then they go on to say, "Be careful, because, when you let your guard down, they use you. You think you have one of them for a friend and all they want to do is to use you." I had never experienced this, but this supposed lunch appointment was such an out-of-the-ordinary occurrence that my mind was searching for every plausible explanation for what was transpiring, and why.

With these words of warning surfacing in my mind, I answered the gate guard emphatically, adding the Arabic word for "no" for more emphasis, "La. La. No. No. Me, no appointment. La!" He frowned, and shook his head in resolute disagreement as he left.

In the meantime, one of the other teachers came into my classroom and told me, "There's some kind of commotion going on out at the front gate. Two Sudanese ladies are here to collect you and take you somewhere. They are not happy that you aren't coming out of the school to meet with them." She added, "Who are they, anyway?"

"I have no idea who they are."

With an ominous tone in her voice, she said, "I'd be careful if I were you. You aren't really going to go somewhere with them, are you?"

"We'll see," was the best reply I could muster up.

In five minutes, flanked by a gate guard on either side of him, the head guard entered my classroom and roared, "Women here. You!" He meant business.

I'd gotten spooked by the other teacher's warning so this time I added a little lie, "La! No appointment! I have meeting. Important meeting today. One hour meeting." The tension in my room had amped up several decibels. I was edgy and the gate guards were edgy, but they made an exit from my room.

Twenty minutes later, the three gate guards returned and entered my classroom with triumphant smiles. They handed me a note scrawled in shaky printing. (All Arabic-trained printing looks shaky when the writer is writing in English because there are absolutely no similarities in the two languages.) It was written in broken English, with numerous misspellings and grammatical errors, in blue ink on a scrap of flimsy brown, paper towel. The following words were written in this format:

Dear Anilla
good afternoon
we are coming now and

we know yu have
meeting-no problem
we are waiting you
to 3:00 an we call
many friends
to meet
you an we make
lunch invitation and
very necessary
your attended.
uou must come
Don't worry-again
we are wating
you
No problem.
Don't worry.

Despite their written assurances, I was worried. Very worried. It was 2:00. Since I didn't really have a meeting I had gained a precious hour to think this through, and make a final decision. The biggest stumbling block, as I saw it, was that there was no back entrance, and there was no slipping in or out of my school. There was only one exit, and that was through the front gate which was guarded by a group of closely-knit gate guards.

At 2:55 I took a deep breath, and I decided to go. One of my considerations was that I needed the protection of the gate guards at my school. I knew I could never save face with them if I didn't leave with the Sudanese ladies because they, for whatever reason, were convinced that I was supposed to go to this appointment. For all I knew, the guards were in cahoots with these ladies and all of them were part of a nefarious scheme to capture me. If that was true, and they were really out to get me, then sooner or later they'd accomplish their goal and get me.

I was feeling trepidation, but there was a calling from a deeper place inside me that was urging me to go! Step into the unknown.

As I walked out of the gate to my school, and climbed into the waiting taxi, all twenty gate guards had apparently been informed of the situation because they each wore a smug look, as if to say, Yes, now you are being a good girl and you are doing exactly what daddy told you to do.

Off I went, in the usual cloud of Khartoum desert dust, scrunched in the backseat of a typical small rickety taxi, with two silent female Sudanese escorts--neither of whom spoke a word of English--seated on either side of me. I had no idea whatsoever where we were going.

The taxi traveled mile, after mile, after mile. I lost all sense of direction. I didn't know if we were going north, south, east, or west, but I knew I was a long way from home. I had never seen this part of Khartoum, and I had never seen these women. But I had seen this part of myself. I was scared. Really scared. Many possibilities went through my mind in rapid succession including: I am being kidnapped and I will be tortured and killed; they want to hold me in captivity and observe my strange foreigner ways; this could prove to be one of the most dangerous, or stupidest, or one of the most interesting adventures of my life, or something in between; I don't know what's going to happen to me.

Finally I decided if this was going to be my last ride anywhere in my life, I might as well sit back and relax. At that point I relaxed as much as one can relax when one doesn't know one's fate while riding in a taxi which has all of its windows open, desert wind and sand are swirling through the cab, it's 125 degrees and there is no air conditioner inside the cab. The streets were full of ruts and we jostled, jerked, and bounced our way at top speed to our unknown destination.

The taxi driver was silent. The women were silent. I was silent.

After at least an hour's ride, the taxi stopped beside an enormous, sprawling, three-story cement house with at least 3,000 square feet on each level. There was a well-kept, huge, formal garden behind the house with a variety of roses and palm trees, as well as green grass. It looked like a pricey, man-made oasis, but I still had no idea where in heaven's name I was.

My two escorts led me inside the front door which was also huge, about eight feet across, and there stood two or three dozen Muslim women decked out in beautiful tobes made of fancy, bright fabrics. They all turned toward me, smiled broadly, and applauded for a good two minutes.

I had no idea why they were applauding. I had no idea who they were. I had no idea who I was to them.

When their applauding stopped, one lady began walking toward me and much to my utter relief I recognized her. I'd met her at a mosque, where I had prayed for several hours in the upstairs section with the women, when I spent a weekend in Omdurman with my friend Fatima's family. I spoke with her briefly that day; she introduced herself as the leader of the Education Committee for the women of that mosque, and she informed me that I was the first Westerner who had ever been invited into their mosque.

Now, the other women listened while their leader, who spoke fairly good English, explained to me that this group of ladies meets every Wednesday afternoon and evening. On this particular Wednesday, I was their guest of honor at a traditional feast of exactly forty foods that had been prepared in my honor. We then dined together. The food was absolutely delicious; as usual, I couldn't recognize anything I was eating other than the fava-bean foul and the baba ganoush.

After the feast we moved into another room where we all sat in a circle on a grass mat on the floor. These devout women were Sufis. (Sufis are the mystics of the Muslim religion.) They sang their ancient songs exalting the prophet Muhammad for two hours as incense billowed from a red clay pot in the center of the circle. The longer they sang the more ecstatic they became, shouting praises to Allah, kissing me on the cheeks and lips, and trilling in the characteristic Arab woman's way. I was fed fresh fruit salad out of a communal, silver bowl by a silver spoon. One woman pulled me, along with the billowing incense pot, under the extra fabric of her canary-yellow and sequined tobe. Inside her tent-like tobe, now thick with smoking incense, she kissed me and hugged me with the strongest, most passionate yet nonsexual, pure and sacred energy I have ever felt, and I was swept away by the intense state of devotion in the room. After I emerged from under her tobe I, too, was swaying, singing, and in an increasingly heightened state of devout and spiritual love.

In a few moments I reached an ecstatic state, and the oldest woman in the circle who had gray hair and long, deep scars running down the length of each of her brown cheeks--the scarring is a traditional rite of passage among Sudanese tribes, but the custom is dying out now--that oldest and wisest woman recognized and honored my state by looking directly at me and nodding, slowly, to me. I slowly nodded back to her, and she took off her emerald-green prayer-bead necklace from her neck and flung it to me from across the circle. As I caught her beads in mid-air she blew kisses to me, and I blew kisses back to her. I pulled the necklace over my head, and I wore it home that evening as I rode in a brand-new, cushy Land Cruiser driven by a husband of one of the women with whom I had feasted and prayed. On the ride home I was in a silent state of ecstatic love which exists whenever we are at one with our God, and thus at one with our self, and therefore at one and at peace with all beings. This love transcends all words and all boundaries.

Chapter 34

KILIMANJARO
CLOSE CALL

We began to lose altitude over Mount Kilimanjaro. From my window seat I watched us descend toward to the highest mountain in Africa which became more beautiful the nearer we got. But within minutes we were dangerously close.

I scanned the faces of the other passengers on the plane, and that included all the teachers from our school. We were flying from Nairobi, Kenya, to Dar es Salaam, Tanzania, where we were to attend the East African Teachers' Conference. All facial expressions were somber, alarmed, and tense.

I checked my seat belt to make sure it was fastened, and quickly reread the emergency procedures. Just then our pilot informed us, via the loud speaker, that we were making a U-turn and heading back to Nairobi on one engine. I began to hold a silent prayer vigil as a din commenced and nearly every Muslim on the plane began to audibly recite verses from the Koran.

As I gazed out the window, I watched us moving ever so slowly through the air and ever so close to the ground; I could clearly see Africans herding their animals. The tension in the cabin rose as did the volume of the prayers. I struck up a hushed conversation with the steward. He confided to me that the pilot had repeatedly made requests for this particular airplane to be grounded because it was unsafe to fly. His requests had gone for naught. This did not help my state of mind.

The Koran recitation on that flight reminded me of a difficult flight I'd experienced in Colombia when the pilot had made an error in judgment and overshot the runway. He crammed on the brakes extra hard, and everything stowed anywhere on the plane went slamming down the aisles or flying through the air. All the passengers ducked for cover and simultaneously all the Roman Catholics, which was almost everyone on that plane, began crossing themselves while audibly praying the rosary over and over. We all made it out alive and unscathed, but just barely. The plane had come to a stop inches before the end of the runway which bordered on a thick, green, wild jungle.

I was hoping and praying that I would live through this flight as well. As our plane approached the Nairobi airport we were very near to the ground. I heard muffled crying and sobbing. Some of the recitations became more plaintive, others were strong and clear. As our plane began taxiing down the runway it was vibrating violently and making deafening, screeching sounds. We came to a halt close to several truck-like contraptions with red lights flashing on their roofs. Standing beside these vehicles were men wearing bulky spacesuits; they looked like creatures out of a science fiction movie. All the men held long hoses which were coming out of the sides of the trucks. While the men in the specialized suits did only God knows what, we were held captive on the plane for two-and-a-half hours without water, food, or a working toilet.

In the middle of the night, amidst the protests of several of our teachers who'd had enough adventure for one evening and wanted to hole up for the night in a Nairobi hotel, we were transferred to another plane. We took off for Dar es Salaam again, this time on a different aircraft. At 1 a.m. we arrived safely, but we were met with difficulties of a different variety.

Those of us carrying U.S. passports were told that we could not exit the Dar es Salaam airport until we paid U. S. $50.00; it was either that or turn around and go back to where we'd come from. Those with passports from the Philippines were told they had to pay $15.00. The Sudanese were told to pay $5.00. We all knew that these fees were arbitrary and assessed on the spot. If we'd come through the same airport the night before, or the following night, the airport tax would have been assessed differently and just as arbitrarily.

I began to feel irritated as I forked over my $50.00, but I coached myself to relax and stop being grumpy about the injustice, that it was simply another example that life isn't fair. Our group then exited the airport, and walked onto the street where all of Dar es Salaam seemed to be in a state of hustle and desperation. Sadly, Dar had seen much better days including the year I resided there when it was a pleasant, relaxed, safe, friendly city fragrant with the scent of tropical flowers and buoyant with hope. All of which provided me with yet one more opportunity to remind myself that the choice is clear: get stressed or don't get stressed. Either way, the outer circumstances aren't changing.

As for our flight with engine trouble, I will never know what saved the day. Pilot expertise? Men-in-spacesuits proficiency? Koran recitations? Christian prayers? An amalgamation of all? Nevertheless, I remain eternally thankful that the day was saved.

Chapter 35

KOFTA, SHWERMA, FOUL, KARKADAY, AND MORE

Everyone at home always asks me, "What do you eat and drink in Khartoum?"

Here's the answer to that question, but first you need to know that there is precious little prepackaged food of any kind, nearly all canned drinks are nonexistent, bottled water does not exist, sanitary restaurants are scarce, and alcoholic beverages are illegal.

Sudan is the largest country on the African continent, and approximately half of Sudan consists of nothing but desert. Vast, harsh Sahara desert. Not much of Sudan is arable. The food supply is dependent on the waters from the Nile River, and Khartoum is positioned on the confluence of the Blue Nile and the White Nile. For the record, the Blue Nile is blue-gray and the White Nile is a silvery-white, thus their names. Both of the Niles flood during the rainy months of July, August, and September when Khartoum is a sopping-wet mess with sewers overflowing, and dirt roads all over the city turning to the consistency of porridge.

Starting in mid-September and continuing through May, the waters of the Nile progressively recede under the desert sun. This leaves a flat surface of rich soil alongside the Nile where crops are planted today, just as they have been planted for centuries. Men dressed in white jalabeyas plow the soil and plant the fields by hand.

In peak season there are plenty of tomatoes, green peppers, onions, garlic, cauliflower, and jer-jer which is a green vegetable similar in taste and appearance to arugula. There is also an abundance of beets, melons, romaine, peas, string beans, fresh mint, potatoes, mangoes, cucumbers that are short and dark-green as well as long and light-green, and radishes that are short and red as well as long and white.

Eggplants are easy to come by and inexpensive. Baba ganoush is a traditional favorite, and made from roasted eggplant which is peeled and then mashed with olive oil, a generous squeeze of fresh lemon, and several dollops of tahina (pronounced tahini in the U.S.) which is a paste-like spread made out of ground sesame seeds. I adore baba ganoosh and never tire of eating it.

As for fruit, bananas and limes are plentiful and excellent. Limes are pronounced lee-moan (accent on moan) which sounds like it would be a cross between a lime and a lemon, doesn't it? In actuality there are a preponderance of limes, but I've never seen a lemon here. If you love grapefruit, you'd love Sudan. Even if you don't love grapefruit, you'd love the grapefruit here. I was not a grapefruit lover until I came to Khartoum, and now I can't get enough of them. The grapefruits are pink, huge, juicy, sweet, cheap, and plentiful. Prime grapefruit season is all year long. I invented an imaginative, tasty treat made of freshly squeezed grapefruit juice which I pour into my blender along with locally-made strawberry yogurt. I also throw in a handful of ice cubes, and whirl it up. It's a frothy, pretty pink, delectable, grapefruit-strawberry, cool, refreshing and welcome beverage in this hot dry desert town.

Watermelon, three times the size of a U.S. football, are also always in season. If you're lucky you can find one that is juicy and crimson-red inside. Usually you're unlucky, and you have to throw it out because it's white and pithy inside.

The variety of produce in Khartoum isn't what it is at home, but when it's available you can count on all of it being freshly picked and succulent.

Along with an abundance of in-season fruits and vegetables there is plenty of rice, lentils, tea, beans, peanuts, olives, halwah (pronounced halvah in the U.S.) and bread. I buy and eat all of these items with the exception of the bread; it has the taste and texture of Wonder Bread which

119

is far from my favorite. Scrumptious baklava sells for the equivalent of $1.50 a kilo--everything here is weighed and sold in kilos. The local feta cheese is wonderfully tangy and tasty; it's also unpasteurized so a lot of people have warned me not to eat it. I eat it anyway, because it's one of the few tasty culinary items which is readily available.

When I first arrived I was using every spare moment settling in to my life in Khartoum, and learning the curriculum I was teaching. To save time, I asked my household worker to buy my produce. Here is the list, verbatim, of the food he bought for me one day, along with the price he paid in Sudanese dinars:

2 cucumbers 500
2 ½ kilos bananas 1,250
8 grapefruit 1,500
8 oranges 1,500
1 ½ kilos lemons 750
2 kilos potatoes 3,000
2 bunches green onion 400
1 bunch carrots 500
2 eggplant 400
2 bunches jer-jer 200
1 plastic sack garlic 500
total 10,500 dinars

He bought all of that produce for a little more than $5.00 dollars in U.S. currency and, as you can see from these prices, the inflation here is horrendous.

Drinkable water takes daily preparation and time. To avoid the risk of contracting water-born diseases, I boil my water for a minimum of twenty minutes to sterilize it and make it safe for drinking. Dehydration is another threat in this dry desert climate. I carry water with me whenever I leave my apartment. Even though water is accessible, if you are a foreigner with a foreign stomach, and you drink water straight from the tap, it will most likely kill you. That's the honest truth.

Fresh eggs are plentiful. They need to be soaked in bleach before cooking them. In fact, it is advisable to wash all eggs, fruits, and vegetables thoroughly, then soak them in bleach, followed by a good rinse in previously boiled water before cooking and eating them. Although I don't like the possibility of ingesting residual bleach, this practice greatly decreases exposure to the many communicable diseases that are rampant in Sudan. It's a matter of taking your pick between the lesser of the evils, and I've made my choice.

As for purchasing prepared food in Khartoum, you can forget it. As for fast food, there are two clones that deserve mention because they have decent-tasting food that doesn't usually give you dysentery; and in Khartoum the latter is more important than the former. Pizza Hot--Hot is not a misspelling--serves tasty, grilled, chicken shwerma. A dollar will buy you a sandwich made of chunks of grilled chicken stuffed inside white bread which has been spread with tahina and shata. Shata is a hot sauce made from fresh, very hot, little, green peppers. Since I love fiery-hot food, discovering Sudanese shata has been a real bonus for me. Deluk Pizza--Deluk is not a misspelling--is within walking distance from my apartment, and their $3.00 vegetarian pizza is fairly decent. However, waiting for it to be prepared and cooked can prove to be a test of one's patience. The place isn't air conditioned and it must be 125 degrees in that hot box of an over-the-counter, take-out kitchen.

In the late afternoon the aroma of foul drifts through the city. Foul is made from fava beans that have been cooked for hours with local spices. It is the most traditional and standard of all of the Sudanese foods because fava beans are both plentiful and cheap, and thus very accessible. Foul is cooked all day throughout Khartoum in kitchens in private homes, or in large aluminum pots over open flames along the sides of dusty, dirty streets by groups of household workers for their personal consumption, or by street vendors in front of little shops with lime-green metal doors. I don't eat foul made by street vendors because the aluminum that has leached into the foul from their cooking pots has got to be at dangerous levels, and I would be taking my life into my hands eating anything made by street vendors because the bacteria count is bound to be high. I have eaten foul numerous times when I've been a guest in Sudanese homes, and I love it. If you love well-seasoned cooked beans, you'd love foul, too.

I'm very fond of the traditional and national drink called karkaday. It's a tea made from dried hibiscus flowers, is rich in vitamin C, and is a gorgeous crimson-red.

Another traditional and delicious Sudanese food is kofta. It's served as an entrée and is the Sudanese version of a meatball, or sausage, depending on who shapes it. It's made of ground beef, bread, and spices all rolled up and baked in the oven. It's scrumptious.

I constantly have to remind myself not to leave a trace of any food or drink anywhere in my apartment, not even a scrap of a grapefruit peeling. If I do, the ants are sure to come marching. They are a constant bother as they advance relentlessly towards their objective, no matter how miniscule the portion. And they bite! Their pin-prick bites don't bother most people after the initial sting, but not me. I'm allergic to the ant bites. They swell to the size of a small orange, itch, and ache, turn bright red, and become very hot. Not fun at all. Thus, Sudanese ants have trained me to be fastidious in my kitchen.

I will close with a food horror story. When I first arrived in Khartoum, I wondered where I could buy raw chicken, or any type of raw meat. I hadn't seen any butcher shops. Then I heard a meat-associated horror story from a husband and wife who teach in our school. They told me, "When we first arrived, we looked high and low for a butcher shop where we could buy decent, non-rancid meat and we finally found one. But, a few months after we'd been buying meat there, we stopped at the shop unexpectedly and caught the butcher spraying Raid on his meat. At that moment we knew why his meat was the only meat in town not covered with flies!" This story dissuaded me from wanting to step foot in a Sudanese butcher shop, ever.

I eat heaps of fresh, succulent fruits and vegetables every day. I'm thriving and healthy because of the amount of fresh produce I consume and also, since I don't have a car, I walk a lot. Along with that, prepackaged junk food and sweets can't be found in the stores. I've never been a big fan of junk food, but I do have a fondness for desserts. Baklava is one of my favorites, but I rarely eat it because the one and only bakery that has baklava is located on the other side of Khartoum and it's not easy to get to. Built-in limitations that ensure healthy living and eating have their advantages. I've lost ten pounds and I feel great.

Author's note: When I was living in Sudan it was the largest country on the African continent. When South Sudan was formed, Sudan became the third largest African country.

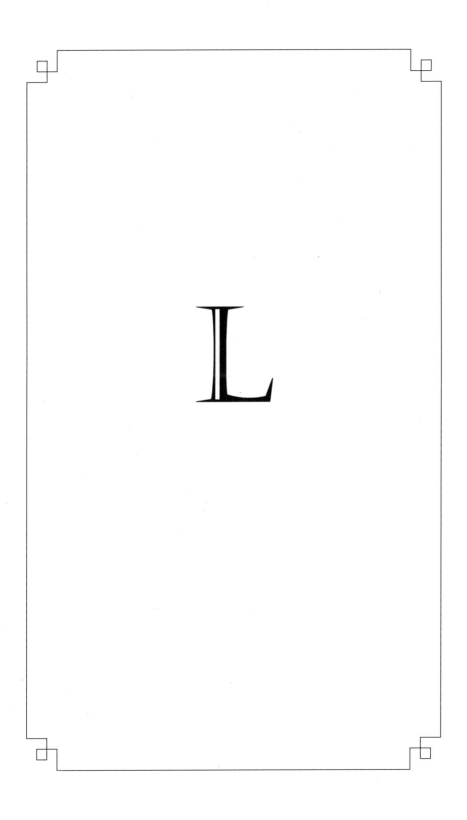

Chapter 36

LETTERS HOME

I believe that life is a matter of attitude. Thus, I don't like to complain. Every once in a while I vent, and this is one of those times. It has to do with sending letters home.

There is no email access in Khartoum, and there are no mail boxes. The nearest post office is a three-mile trudge along the dirt shoulder of a dusty, dirty, eight-lane arterial called Africa Road by some, and Airport Road by others. I have no idea why this street has two names; most of the streets in Khartoum have no names at all. Cars, trucks, and buses barrel down Africa/Airport Road honking their horns madly while they dodge and dart around each other with inches to spare. I always make the trip in the daylight because there are so many potholes. If I were to walk after dark I would risk disappearing into one of those potholes, and vanishing. This means I have to make the trip in the blazing sun. The sun coupled with whizzing vehicles, honking horns, and thick clouds of dust make for an unsavory walking experience.

When I finally step up to the worn, wooden counter at the post office, I have to hope that the clerk understands what I need because he only speaks Arabic. On top of all of this, I can't be sure that any of my letters are going to reach any of my friends because the mail system here is described by everyone as "only fairly reliable." This means that there is a good chance that my letters won't ever make it to their intended destination.

A fellow teacher tipped me off to another way of sending letters home. This entails keeping an ear to the ground for an expat who is journeying back to the States, arranging with that person to take my letters home and mail them from inside the States. This procedure has all kinds of obvious hassles including restrictions on the amount the letters can weigh. So I've devised an intricate system wherein I give the expat five letters which are mailed to key people, and then those five people make copies and mail that letter to five more of my friends, and so on, and so on; eventually everyone receives my letter. But, so far I've only been able to find one person who was leaving for the States and who was willing to mail the five letters for me.

What's more, I don't like to write letters longhand because it's so time-consuming, but the only available computer is located in our school's computer lab and it's frequently not available. Get the picture? It's been a hassle all the way around.

Guess what happened a few days ago. At my school, on the administrative assistant's desk, I noticed a stack of letters and they were all addressed to the United States. Upon inquiring I was told that I can buy stamps from the assistant, put those stamps on my letters, deposit my letters in a gray, plastic basket in the main office, and the assistant mails all of those letters a couple of times every week. That's a fine thing to find out eight months after my arrival. I was fuming when I discovered that mailing letters could have been so simple. Ah well, at least I won't have any more wilted trudges down Africa-Airport Road.

Author's note: This vignette was written in 1997 when my only means of communicating with loved ones at home was through letters sent via the postal system, or phone calls made on scarce landlines. This narrative serves as a reminder to appreciate the ease and efficiency in communication that modern technology has brought us.

Chapter 37

LOST IN THE LOCAL SHOPPING MALL

Take a moment to picture yourself in your local shopping mall.

Now I'm going to take you on a shopping trip in Khartoum. Get ready to be astonished. The only similarity between the two is the money paid when an item is purchased.

Souk el-Shabi is Khartoum's equivalent of a U.S. shopping mall. Souk is the Arabic word for market. El-Shabi means public market, and one of its characteristic features is that its proprietors must offer a decent price to customers.

One Saturday I, along with two good friends, a Scot and a Brit, meandered down the uneven dirt lanes of Souk el-Shabi. We strolled past tiny, rectangular shops with dirt floors. Each shop had a lime-green metal door and a male proprietor who called out, "Itfadalay!" which means, Welcome! or, You are welcome here.

The shops were all a uniform size and big enough inside for two medium-sized customers, one shopkeeper, and a little bit of merchandise. Due to the small square footage, each specializes in one commodity. The clothing shops for little girls overflowed with stiff frills and lace. Women's dresses were a blend of flimsy polyester and cotton; most of them were printed with tacky roses and butterflies, with extra-gaudy glitter and a scattering of kitschy hearts. As usual, there was nothing for sale that I would have wanted to wear. The three of us walked by most of those shops, and stayed focused on our errands. I was shopping for lentils, Helen for a dress, and Shane for cotton stuffing for pillows.

I found a mound of orange lentils inside a woven basket set on a rough, wooden table. I scooped a small handful of lentils into my hand and inspected them. They were dusty, but they weren't dirty. Dust is to be expected because anything and everything gets dusty after it's been out in the Khartoum air for more than a couple of minutes. There were small, gray stones mixed with the lentils which meant I'd have to pick out the stones or risk breaking a tooth, but I'd certainly seen worse. After bargaining a little, I struck a deal with the shopkeeper's son, a young man in his late teens with smooth, chocolate-brown skin and large, deep-brown, dreamy eyes. I paid him 5,000 Sudanese dinars for two kilos of orange lentils which amounted to about $1.25 a kilo in U.S. dollars. I leaned toward my friends saying, "I'll make a lentil, tomato, eggplant, and garlic stew with these, and I'll invite you two over to help me eat it."

Helen wanted a new dress because the embroidery was starting to tear on all her favorites. We searched high and low until we found the one and only shop with the particular style of Indonesian dress Helen liked to wear. When we finally came upon it, Shane and Helen were walking a step or two ahead of me. They disappeared behind a row of women's dresses hanging in front of that shop. There wasn't room for me inside. I stood outside and poked my head between the dresses so I could see what was going on. Shane stood next to Helen as she looked through the choices. We both encouraged her to buy the yellow dress with the brown embroidery. After some bargaining, Helen settled on 20,000 Sudanese dinars, a decent price.

Next was Shane's turn. She was shopping for a friend of hers who needed cotton suitable for stuffing inside of homemade pillows, lots and lots of pillows. We found a shop that made mattresses, and Shane bought twenty-seven kilos of homegrown, cotton stuffing which the shopkeeper crammed into a dirty, brown, burlap bag with bursting seams. I was appointed to keep an eye on the sack of cotton puffs while Helen and Shane went to fetch the car.

I'd been standing next to the bag, which came up to my waist, for several minutes, when the shopkeeper, who had little tuffs of white cotton in his hair and ears, walked next door to a tiny restaurant which was serving Pepsi, coffee and tea. There he borrowed a small, metal-framed chair. As he set it down next to me, he gestured graciously and said, "Itfadalay!"

I smiled as I said, "Shukrun," and I sat down in the chair.

As I waited thirty-five minutes for Helen and Shane to return, the sparse nylon strings which made-up the seat of the chair, gave way more and more. I sank lower, and lower, and the metal frame hugged my sweaty body closer, and closer. While it collapsed around me, I figured what goes around comes around. Earlier in the day I'd been looking with a judgmental eye at those "tacky" designs on the women's clothes, but in reality I was the one who looked tacky.

There I sat, in my sinking seat and collapsing chair, sweating mightily while dressed in a faded, beige, saggy, cotton-knit skirt and an unsightly cotton top. The sage-green top had looked nice and new when I arrived in Khartoum, but my household worker had somehow managed to splatter bleach on it, resulting in irregular, tiny, white spots all across the front. (I subsequently fired the worker as a result of numerous household catastrophes. For example, he insisted that he wash my household dishes in his bucket of filthy mop water which I discovered only because I was at home and very sick with a stomach ailment, and I happened to stumble into the kitchen when he was washing the dishes in the mop water.)

Why, you might ask, did I continue to wear that shapeless skirt and grubby top? My rationale was that I would only wear this getup on occasions when I would be in the company of good, accepting friends in situations when I'd end up sweaty, wrinkled, and dirty. Besides, the entire outfit was very soft and well suited to the desert heat, and there wasn't anything in Khartoum I could buy similar to it. Along with this gauche attire, I was sporting comfortable, tan Birkenstock sandals on my size eleven feet which must have looked like a Stone Age throwback to the Sudanese people because Sudanese women wear stylish high heels on their feet, at all times. Yes, I was the tacky one.

Add to this scene the fact that I was the only female in sight, and the only person with white skin. From my saggy seat, I could see approximately one-hundred brown and black-skinned men. Now you understand why, for thirty-five minutes, the Sudanese men and I looked at each other while I waited for Shane and Helen. No one pointed at anyone, no one gazed for more than five or ten seconds at a time, and no one burst out laughing. But we did look. My white skin signified to them that I came from a prosperous country. I figured they were wondering why I would want to look so tasteless when I could buy, and wear, high heels and polyester dresses covered with glitzy butterflies, roses, and hearts.

Knowing the Sudanese as I did, I surmised that they would have been curious as they looked at me, but not judgmental, and that's a big difference. Knowing this made me feel even worse about having judged the Sudanese women's clothes earlier in the afternoon. My attitude began to sink because I knew I was an example of the expression: When you point your finger, a thousand fingers point back at you.

Meanwhile, as Shane and Helen explained to me later, the two of them had gotten lost trying to find the car because there weren't any distinguishing characteristics to guide them along row after row of narrow, dirt streets lined with hundreds of tiny shops. They couldn't figure out which look-alike lane they'd parked on.

When they finally found the car a swarm of beggars pressed their hungry hands against the car windows while demanding, "Baksheesh." Shane was too afraid to drive away for fear of injuring one of the beggars. Finally, she inched her car out of its parking spot, made her getaway, and arrived to pick up the cotton and me. By that time my sense of humor had revived, and I was chuckling at how ridiculous I looked in my sagging chair and tatty clothes.

We got lost as we attempted to pick our way to the main thoroughfare. Shopkeepers pointed us in the correct direction, and pulled their chairs from the front of their shops inside their shops so we could squeeze by in our slow-moving car. After about fifteen minutes of bumping and creeping along narrow dirt lanes lined with small shops and turning right and left, and left and right, again and again, I spied the main street at the end of a little pathway. I yelled, "Shane! Stop! I see it! Our street is out there!" Shane stomped on her brakes, backed up, turned a sharp left, drove down a final, rutted lane of Souk el-Shabi, merged onto the dirt thoroughfare, and headed home.

Next time you're on a shopping trip in your local shopping mall, don't take it for granted.

Chapter 38

LOST IN THE VAST SAHARA

Our heretofore reliable driver and navigator got us abysmally lost in the vast Sahara desert on a trip back to Khartoum from the Red Sea. To give you an idea of how unpopulated that desert is, in ten hours of driving we saw a total of fifteen people, and we wouldn't have seen them had it not been for the fact that we searched them out. But I'm getting ahead of myself.

It wasn't entirely the fault of our driver and navigator that we were lost. We were crossing a stretch of desert where there weren't any roads. We followed railroad tracks and sparse beacons, as tall as mini-skyscrapers, that marked the railroad. We got lost when the tracks vanished in a sea of desert sand. The relentless wind had blown barrels of sand over the tracks, and the beacons became invisible due to sand swirling in the air. Lost in the vast desert we were in desperate need of directions. Our only hope was to get that information from locals, and the only locals who lived around there were nomads. Without the help of nomads we would most likely perish.

Our guides had abided by the guidance in the saying, "Pray to Allah but tie your camel first," when they stacked containers of both gas and water on top of our two vehicles before we embarked on the desert crossing. Nonetheless, no matter how much extra gas and water one has, it only lasts for just so long. Several containers of gas won't get you very far in the Sahara's vastness because it's almost as big as the entire United States, and a few extra jugs of water are laughably finite juxtaposed to the Sahara's unrelenting desert sun; it's purported to be the hottest desert on the earth. Prayers can and do work miracles, but our survival was at stake and a heavy feeling permeated our Land Rover as we drove through the unending desert searching for nomads who could point the way. We did find several nomad camps, but each of the crudely built huts had been vacated. Our translator explained in broken English to me, "When water source dry, nomad take camel and family and move, search for water in different location." It did not bode well for us that this section of desert did not currently have water, and the longer we searched for nomads the more gas we were using.

I couldn't bear to look at my watch during that agonizing search. After what seemed like a couple of hours, we came upon a nomad camp with three adults and a dozen children. Noticeable relief was in the air in our Land Rover, but there was terror in the eyes of the nomad children. They were immobilized, frozen with fear as they watched us get out of our two vehicles. I looked to our translator for an explanation and he said, "I hear children talk. Children see you, white skin people for first time. They scared. Think maybe you ghost."

Our guide, driver, translator and the nomads all had African features and dark skin. But, there were six of us who had white, Northern European skin tones and light-brown to very blonde hair; and these nomad children didn't have an inkling that white-skinned people existed in the world. No wonder they were so afraid of us.

I soon realized that there was yet another reason why the children were frightened. I witnessed their father who, having decided that the children had been outside of their hut long enough, menacingly picked up a handful of rocks and threatened to throw the rocks at the children if they didn't obey him and get back inside their hut. Judging from the looks on the faces of the kids, they had been hit by those rocks before. How sad.

The children were wearing the most inventive and odd hairdos I've ever seen. For example, one of them had her head shaved bald except for long bangs which were twisted into several, looped, black braids; she also had long, looped braids at the nape of her neck. I'm guessing that my blondish, semi-curly hair, blown into a mess by the strong wind, must have looked really weird to them because evaluations regarding outward appearances usually are reciprocal.

One of the girls, who looked to be about twenty years old, darted across the sand on all fours and sprang onto a boulder where she sat on her haunches and stared at us with eerie, wild eyes. She repeated this pattern over and over. She'd perch for a few minutes on a boulder, spring to another boulder, and land on it on all fours where she'd stare at us again. Her dress billowed crazily in the desert wind while she darted, pounced and perched. She kept her distance from us, and from the nomad and the children. I wondered if she could be a true, feral child.

After an involved verbal exchange in Arabic between the father, and our guide and drivers, accompanied by much hand gesturing, our translator looked at me and said, "We go now. We trust direction from nomad? We no know. We hope correct."

I thought, Uh oh, they're not sure we can trust the directions the nomads gave us.

I was worried. Our driver and navigator looked worried. They talked intently as we set out again. Trying to make up for lost time, our drivers drove at a fairly high speed over the floor of the bumpy desert, and my kidneys felt as if they were going to be forever loosened from their moorings.

We got stuck in the sand three times that afternoon. Getting stuck in the sand is another constant threat to desert travel. We got irrevocably stuck once that day, and we were pulled out by our companion vehicle. This is an example of why it is highly advisable to travel with another vehicle. In this case, the Land Cruiser pulled us out in less than fifteen minutes. Later that afternoon we had another mishap. We drove up and over a large bulge of sand at high speed, flew airborne, and landed in an unexpected and rather deep hole. Everything that had been packed in the rear of our Land Rover slammed forward. A full suitcase walloped me on the back of my neck and head, causing my forehead to whack the front seat, which brought tears of pain to my eyes. My head hurt horribly, but at least our trusty Land Rover was still running.

The last several hours we traveled in the dark. We'd lost precious time when we were wandering around looking for nomads. The less time one needs to travel at night in a desert the better because travelers can quickly get disoriented and swallowed up in the darkness. There was an audible sigh of relief in my vehicle when we saw the electric lights of a town, our destination, in the distance. We were lost no more, and we knew for sure that the nomads had pointed us in the correct direction. We had been guided to safety. Was it dumb luck that we finally found the nomads, or was it by divine guidance? I know where I stand on the answer to this question, and I said my prayers of thanks that night as I fell into a much-needed and deep sleep.

At the end of that day I understood why camels are such prized beasts of burden. They don't need gas, they can last for fourteen days without water, and they don't get stuck in the sand very often or for very long. I also realized why camels are petulant. It's a tough life in the desert.

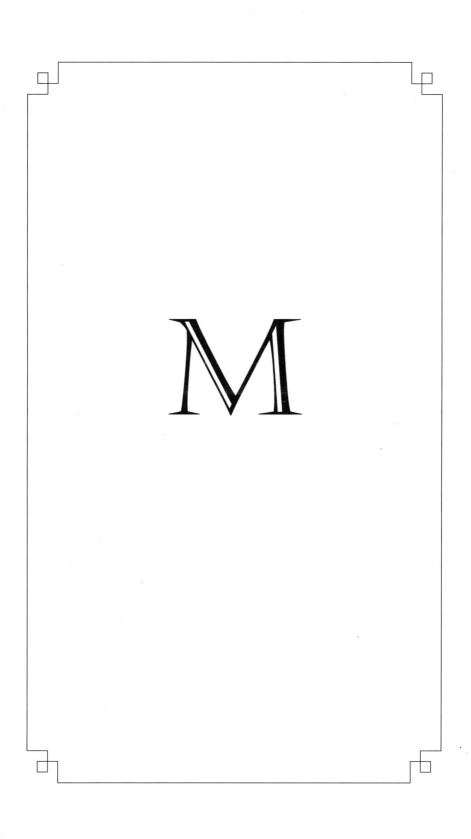

Chapter 39

MEROE'S SECRET

Shh-shh-shh, don't tell anyone about the antiquities at Meroe.

Meroe's pyramids were constructed 2,500 years ago, and so far they are one of the best-kept secrets on the face of our beautiful planet. All is quiet now at Meroe and it is a stretch of the imagination to picture it as a lively Nubian kingdom on the Nile River, active and flourishing until the 4th century A.D. The bustling kingdom and the Nile are nowhere to be seen now.

In Egypt the tourists are packed elbow-to-elbow at the pyramids. Not so in Meroe where it's just you, a few fellow members of the rag-tag Sudan Archeological Society, expanses of desert as far as the eye can see, the constant wind, and a handful of local, relaxed villagers selling their goods to you quite calmly.

The first time I travelled to Meroe from Khartoum, I was with the Sudan Archeological Society which had organized a day trip for about thirty of us. During the two-hour drive north from Khartoum I was relegated to ride in a backwards-facing rear seat in an elongated station wagon. I was too tall for the seat in which I was sitting. I had to scrunch down to avoid hitting my head against the roof, and my knees were jammed against the back of the seat in front of me, causing me a tortuous backache. Fortunately, the backache went away when I began to walk around at our first stop, a magnificent site across the road from Meroe.

We strolled around in the hot sun gawking at the hieroglyphs on the pyramids and the gargoyles in an ancient, underground Roman bath which speaks to the fact that there was enough water here in Roman times to support baths. Today there is no water in sight. There is only parched desert.

As we meandered, we listened to information and explanations given to us by an astute German archeologist and professor. He has dedicated his professional life to the painstaking task of excavating the site, and understanding Meroe and the surrounding vicinity. He provided us with a priceless, in-person, free of charge, audio tour as he explained the significance and the history of on-site relics such as paintings of goddesses and cartouches, incense burners, statues of dogs from the underworld, and tombs of kings and queens with names such as Amanirenas and Natakamani who reigned from roughly 40 B.C. to 20 A.D. during the kingdom of Kush. More recent information included the fact that, in the 1830s, treasures made of gold were found here by the Italians. However, in their notes, the Italians stated that they didn't believe they had really found gold, but rather something that resembled gold.

The most interesting tidbit I gleaned is that there is a constant threat to these pyramids. This threat is the desert itself because a strong wind blows for eight or nine months from the north, and for three or four months from the south. The wind never stops blowing and moving the desert sand. Meroe's pyramids would be buried in one year's time if there weren't workers employed to dig out the sand on a daily basis.

As planned, most of the Archeological Society members returned to Khartoum that afternoon. One adventurous carload of us, actually a Land Cruiser load of us, spent the night at the site. A few people had decent outdoor gear including foam pads. Most of the others bedded down on the desert sand. I found a semblance of a bed consisting of four posts made of tree branches, across which was strung drooping macramé. I dragged it to the vicinity of the others, and I bedded down on it. It was uncomfortable, but it proved to be more comfortable than sleeping on the hard, bare sand.

There I was, bundled up in my sleeping bag, too excited to sleep because I was in the wind-swept Sudanese desert under a sky jam-packed with stars, and lying beside pyramids which were built 2,500 years ago.

After a couple of hours I finally did fall asleep. A short time later a voice whispered, "Hey, is anyone else awake?"

"Yes," I answered, "I'm awake thanks to you for waking me up when you asked, 'Is anyone else awake?'"

That made both of us laugh, and our laughter woke up someone else. The three of us decided to get up and raid the stash of coconut-and-berry cream-filled cookies. As we munched the cookies we giggled under a star-filled sky. After an hour we went back to our beds, such as they were, and fell asleep.

I woke up to a brilliant-red sunrise, and hoisted myself onto my elbows. In the distance I saw two camels and their riders loping toward our campsite. They stopped their camels about thirty meters from us, climbed off, unpacked their saddle bags, spread pieces of faded, cotton cloth on the golden sand, plunked down their wares on the pieces of cloth, and waited for us to rise and shine. Within thirty minutes there were a dozen adult male vendors, five child vendors, four camels, and two mangy dogs patiently waiting for us to shop at their traveling mini-mall.

With the help of my Sudanese friends who had also spent the night at Meroe, I bargained for three silver bracelets shaped like horseshoes with hand-tooled, symmetrical, intricate designs etched on both sides. I also bargained for several small hand-tooled leather amulets. These are commonly worn in Sudan for healing purposes. I had been told that when people have a spiritual, emotional, or physical problem they go to their sheik for council. The sheik writes a verse from the Koran on a piece of paper because it is believed that the intention of the words in that verse will bring the needed healing to the ailing person. That verse is sealed inside an amulet which is worn by the person until the necessary healing takes place. The amulet can then be taken off and sold to a kwaga, the Arabic word for foreigner, such as myself. I also bought a large, hand-carved, dark-brown, wooden bowl on which I spent 30,000 Sudanese dinars, the equivalent of approximately U.S. $16.00, and it would have cost at least 200,000 dinars if I'd bought it in a shop in Khartoum. These goods were sold to me presumably as these traders have sold their merchandise for centuries, bargaining calmly and fairly while displaying their wares on a humble piece of cloth in the sand.

On the drive back to Khartoum I reread the notes I'd taken. As I reviewed the rich twentfour hours I had just experienced, I wondered how many pyramids and remnants of ancient kingdoms remain silently buried beneath thousands of years of blowing sand. Maybe time will tell. The desert certainly isn't telling.

Chapter 40

MORTAR FIRE AND
RAVAGES AT KASSALA

War changes all landscapes including a cluster of intriguingly and oddly shaped mountainous rocks bordering a town named Kassala. The rocks rise up dramatically out of the flat, surrounding terrain. In the past, they attracted hikers and climbers from around the world. Now those mountains are laced with land mines, and war-faring guerillas roam the mountains and launch attacks with mortar fire. Kassala used to be the jumping-off point to catch a bus to Ethiopia or Eritrea. Those borders are now closed due to the war.

I spent twelve hours in Kassala, and I wondered if I'd leave alive.

My five friends and I were travelling in two cars. Kassala was an overnight stop as we headed for our spring-break vacation at the Red Sea. We stopped to show our papers and passports at the police checkpoint at the entrance to Kassala. Next, we were required to check in at the police station inside the city. There we were given an unexpected offer for a police escort into Kassala's mountains, which we accepted. The security officer rode in the car I was seated in. He was about twenty-years-old, very skinny, with a big smile and a sweet disposition. He showed us where to hike, and where not to hike so we could avoid the land mines. As he led us on a trek up the side of a steep mountain, the golden-pink sun was setting, the call to prayer was echoing from the mosques in the city, nearby mortar fire had ceased, and a temporary calm prevailed on our side of the mountains.

No one was allowed to take photographs in Kassala because the city and the surrounding area was a restricted military zone. I was told, in no uncertain terms, I could not take my camera out of my bag. I would have loved to have taken photos, especially of a teenage boy we passed on the road. He was riding on a weathered, wooden cart pulled by a gray donkey and he was wearing the traditional, white jalabeya. On his head, rather than the traditional turban or white skullcap, he sported a Western-style, bright-red, baseball cap with the bill turned toward the back. He was an iconic, visual representation of Western culture encroaching on this part of the world. Albeit slight at this point in time, but one wonders about the eventual influence on the clothes, minds, and spirits of the Sudanese, and others.

That evening we checked into the Hipton Hotel which was the nicest place in town. Hipton, by the way, is not a misspelling and it definitely was not the Hilton. For one night's lodging I paid the equivalent of fifteen U.S. dollars. The Hipton restaurant served the toughest chicken I've ever eaten in my life. Being a city girl, I had no idea chicken could be that tough. Kassala was known all over Sudan for its delicious fruit. Why didn't they serve us any fruit for dinner? Beats me.

I retired to my room after we finished dinner, read, fell asleep, and was awakened at 2:30 a.m. by a rat scooting under the door to my room. It made a beeline, so to speak, across my large room and into an adjoining and smaller room where I'd left a handful of peanuts on a petite, round table. Earlier in the day my travel companions purchased the peanuts from a street vendor, and shared some with me when they noticed me eyeing the peanuts longingly. I do love peanuts, but I hadn't bought any because the woman's hands which were scooping the peanuts into the little bags which she then sold, those hands of hers were downright filthy. I watched my travel companions gobble fistfuls of the peanuts and, since they didn't keel over within three hours of devouring them, I silently decided, What the heck; I'll try some too. Now the rat's radar picked up the scent of peanuts. It sprinted into the small room and chowed down the peanuts while making disgusting cooing, cackling, chattering, and shrill trilling sounds.

Meanwhile, I was remembering a story my grandfather told me about rats. Years ago, I'd asked my grandfather to tell me a story from his war days and he answered me, saying, "Down in those trenches you had to have a buddy you could trust because, when you fell asleep, the rats would take bites from your body's flesh unless your buddy shooed the rats away from you. And then, when your buddy slept, you would shoo the rats away from his body for him. That way, you could get some sleep, and you were safe from the rats."

There I was in Kassala, remembering my grandfather's story about rats in the trenches, and I began to picture that demented-sounding, icky rat tearing into the flesh on my body after it finished the peanuts. I got up, slammed shut the door to that tiny, adjacent room and I threw my large, full, duffel bag in front of the door to block the rat's exit. You'd have thought a bucking bronco had been sequestered in that room from the racket that rat made banging against the door. Then all was quiet. Quiet except for a gnawing sound. I dozed off several times, but continued to wake up because I was afraid the rat would gnaw its way out of the little room and rip into my flesh if I fell asleep.

Then mortar fire began exploding, and it was close! How close I didn't know because I'd never before been in a war. I did know that it was too close for comfort. The explosions were not muffled. Kassala had become an active war zone. I ran to my window and looked outside expecting to see townspeople running for their lives, and I anticipated joining them. I saw no one. I continued to look. I continued to see no one. I thought, Oh my God! This is war! Sudan and Eritrea are fighting and no one is leaving because this is the place they call home. Innocent townspeople don't deserve to be attacked like this. How many people on our earth are going through this tonight? Why? Why?!

My mind and heart were racing. Inside my head I yelled at myself, Calm down! Stop thinking! Now!

I stopped asking unanswerable questions, and focused on taking deep breaths. I managed to compose myself, but between the rat's vicious, masticating noises and the exploding mortars I was awake most of the night. About every hour, or so, I'd walk from my second-floor room down a long, silent hallway, and down a wide flight of stairs to the lobby. I had hopes of finding an attendant at the front desk to assist me on rat patrol, but no one was around.

Just before dawn the explosions subsided, and at about 6:00 a.m. a yawning and sleepy-eyed assistant appeared at the front desk. I beseeched him, in a mixture of mime and sign language because he only spoke Arabic, to get that rat out of my room. He chuckled kindheartedly as I mimed the part of a nasty rat, which made me chuckle, too. Without any hesitation he walked up the stairs to my room with me. I couldn't believe it when, with no second thoughts, he stuck his hand under the door to the adjoining room and felt around. Indicating to me that there was nothing there, he opened the door to the room. There was no rat. Evidently the varmint had found an escape route, but not before it finished off the peanuts. It also gnawed a grapefruit-size hole in my sturdy duffel bag and a half-dollar-size hole in a thick, leather satchel which I'd stowed inside the duffel.

I, too, was in need of escape. I was more than thankful that I had the privilege of leaving Kassala by Land Rover that morning.

Chapter 41

MY TREE HOUSE

My apartment, one-third of which has floor-to-ceiling glass windows and sliding-glass doors, is surrounded by a massive deck and perches atop a three-story house. It was dubbed a "tree house" by the five fourth-grade boys from my school who came to visit me one afternoon, unannounced. (Incidentally, I hadn't told them where I live, and they're not my students. I teach sixth through twelfth graders.) When they discovered the steep, wooden stairs leading to my top-most deck, which literally sits on top of my apartment, the boys yelled, "Hey! Cool! You live in a tree house! How much do you pay?"

I replied, "I don't pay any money for it."

The most precocious of the boys countered, "Cool tree houses cost money. Tell us how much!"

The others chimed in, demanding to know the answer, they yelled, "Yeah! Yeah! Tell us how much!"

I said, "The school pays for it. I get it for free because I teach at the school."

"You're lucky. You're lucky." echoed from one boy to the next.

I agreed with them, saying, "Yes, I am. I'm very lucky."

I offered them Dr. Pepper, which they guzzled. (It's almost impossible to find it here.) They jumped on my mini-trampoline, while yelling, "Hey! Let's pretend we're missiles!" They opened every door, drawer, and cupboard, and they looked at all of my "cool stuff" (that's what they called it) including green and pink rocks I plucked from Sudan's desert, sea shells I gathered on the beaches of sweet Zanzibar Island a few months prior to their visit, and prunes I brought from Seattle.

"Hey!" they shouted, "You're lucky. You have prunes. We love prunes, but you can't get them here!" and so I let them eat some of my prunes.

They demanded to know, "Does anyone sleep in your big bed with you?" I didn't answer that question. It wasn't any of their business if anyone slept in my bed with me, or not.

Not long after they arrived, the boys departed, taking their leave as impetuously as they had appeared.

Most people react as enthusiastically to my apartment as the boys did, in large part because apartments such as mine are unheard of in Khartoum. Extended families live together, and rarely does anyone live separately in a detached unit. Under my large, one-bedroom apartment are two, very large, self-sufficient stories that are connected through an internal stairway that has a door, with locks, at the top of each staircase. Interconnecting levels are the norm here.

My apartment is reached through an external stairway at the top of which is a front door made of metal with a secure, dead-bolt lock on it. The top half of my front door has been fashioned into an abstract design with spaces between the pieces of metal. The spaces are large enough to let me see who is on the other side of the door, and I can decide if I want to unlock the door and let that person in, or not.

The decks are another stunning feature. After entering my front door, one is standing on my main deck which surrounds my apartment on two sides; it could accommodate more than one hundred people seated in chairs. From my living room and kitchen I look onto this deck through glass windows and glass doors. And then there's the topmost deck. It's big enough for me and two handfuls of my friends to catch a bird's eye view of my neighborhood, or gaze at a sizeable portion of the sky.

Whenever anyone from Europe or the United States visits me for the first time they always say, "This is the perfect place for a party." I've hosted a couple of parties on my deck and I do enjoy a good party, but I'm not here to party. I'm here to learn from and embrace this Muslim culture that is virtually inaccessible to U.S. citizens; this is an exceptional opportunity, and I am making the most of it.

Nestling next to the south side of my deck is a big, old, healthy, palm tree. During the warm, dry, winter months its fronds provide a gathering place for flocks of song birds and wild, migratory, yellow canaries, iridescent pink-and-gray doves, and jays with bright-blue topknots and splotches on their side panels as blue as the magnificent Indian Ocean. In the evenings I sit at the east end of my deck and watch the moon as it rises from behind the tall, bushy tree with thousands of little green leaves that grow in the next-door neighbor's yard. Sometimes I sleep outside on my deck under the bright constellations as a friendly breeze ruffles my blankets.

I feel snug and safe perched in my tree house in Khartoum.

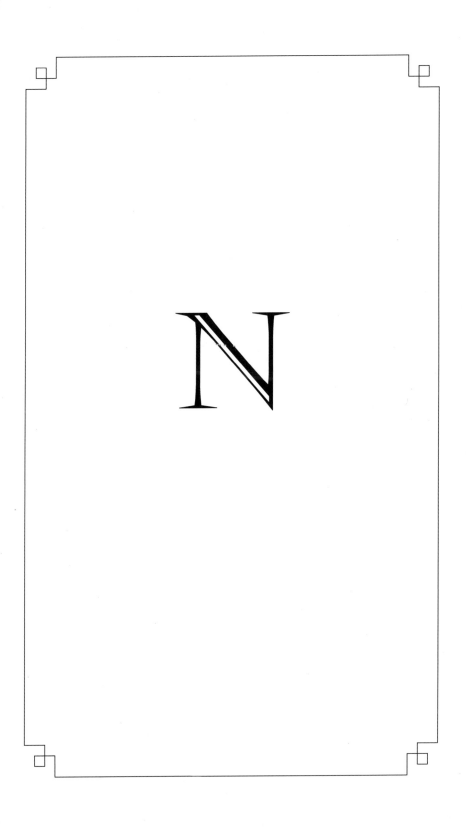

Chapter 42

NEIGHBORLY CHRISTMAS TEA

The Muslim family who lives across the street invited another teacher and me over to their house for a Christmas tea on December 20. It was a tea party like none other. I'll tell you about it in a few paragraphs. I'm beginning with a description of the family's living situation because it is typically Sudanese, and for that reason it's interesting.

This family lives like nearly all Sudanese live with several extended family members packed together under one roof. In their large house, the mother and father sleep in a room next to the living room. The two unmarried daughters sleep in a bedroom adjoining the room where the television is watched, and that room is entered through the kitchen. One of the married sons, his wife and their daughter live in a separate apartment entered by a stairway situated in the driveway. Another married son and his wife live in an apartment that is reached by climbing stairs from the dining room.

There is a formal entrance to the living room in the front of the house. Sara and I entered the house from a side entrance because Sara is friends with the family, and she always enters through the informal, side entry. We were greeted by one of the daughters who escorted us into the T.V. room where we were seated on beds. (It's typical in Khartoum to find yourself sitting on beds, and not couches or chairs.) From our beds, Sara and I watched the T.V. which was tuned to a station showing Mecca with tens of thousands of people walking around the sacred Mecca stone at the Hajj. (More times than not, Mecca and the Hajj are on the T.V. whenever I walk into a home that has a T.V. turned on.)

After about twenty minutes, Sara and I were whisked out of the bedroom and into the living room where the tea party commenced. Our neighbors had invited a handful of their English-speaking friends to the party including a Brit named William who has lived in the Arab world for thirty years, is fluent in Arabic, and is one of the funniest human beings I have ever encountered in my life. Everything he said was witty, hysterically funny, and laced with British intellectual humor. He was dressed impeccably in a navy-blue blazer, matching trousers, dress shirt, and silk ascot, but he was missing his four front teeth which didn't faze him a bit. Figure that one out. I've decided that Khartoum doesn't attract the norm in Western personality types.

For beverages we were served tea, coffee, and exotic fresh fruit drinks. The living room tables were brimming with bowls of freshly roasted peanuts, popcorn, a plethora of expensive European candies, and butter cookies. I ate and drank my fill, and then they brought the food. Did you get that last sentence? I repeat, and then they brought the food: plates of homemade pizzas, five different kinds of fancy layer cakes, strudel, brownies, more cookies, and an endless supply of scrumptious tarts. Actually, all of the food was delicious. From beginning to end the tea party was delightful.

During the tea (which, as you've gathered, was more like a lavish buffet) our neighbors learned that Sara and I were leaving that evening for a vacation in Egypt. They insisted on driving us to the airport. Their offer was a godsend because she and I had planned to hail a taxi on a dirt street which would have meant that we would have arrived at the airport sweaty and dusty. And who wants to take off for Christmas vacation in that condition? We jumped at the invitation to be driven to the airport in their comfy Land Cruiser.

The Christmas tea hosted by Muslims who wanted their European and American friends to feel at home in Khartoum at Christmastime, followed by the ride to the airport, are illustrative examples of Sudanese hospitality. Time after time, Sudanese extended warm, gracious acts of kindness to me. In return, I have promised myself that I will do what I can to help foreigners feel at ease when I return to the U.S. In this way I can give back and contribute to making the world go around with a positive spin.

Chapter 43

NO EASY SUPERMARKET SHOPPING

There is only one supermarket in Khartoum, and I don't go to it. Getting there necessitates a long taxi ride to the other side of town, and their prices are sky high. I shop with the locals in tiny kiosks and small stores for my pre-packaged items, which are mighty scarce, and I go to open-air markets for everything else.

Shopping for anything in Khartoum is an ongoing mystery for me because nothing is located where I expect it to be. Dried hibiscus flowers, which are brewed into tea, are found next to cardamom pods which are next to mounds of frankincense. All of these items are sold at open-air markets, in bulk, by vendors who display their teas, spices, incense, and other goods in jumbled heaps inside of large, hand-made, woven, straw baskets which are placed on wobbly wooden tables.

Incidentally, when you burn the frankincense you place it on chunks of charcoal which you set alight in order to make the frankincense release its powerful aroma. So, I expected the charcoal to be sold in the same place as the incense, or at least in the general vicinity, but it's not. The charcoal is found at the fruit and vegetable stands.

Another good example of shopping surprises is the location of common, everyday envelopes. After looking all over town, I learned that you buy them in teeny kiosks scattered around the city. These tiny booths stock a few paperback books, seemingly less than ten books at any given time, and envelopes. The envelopes are never displayed. They are hidden under the counter, and you have to ask for them.

All of this is a far cry from the ease with which we whiz down the isle of a local supermarket with a well-designed shopping cart, pluck items off the shelves and place them in a cart, proceed through the ever-so-streamlined checkstand, and off we go. But where else would fellow shoppers gather around me, and smile, and applaud politely and enthusiastically while I bravely attempt to speak Arabic. And where else would honest, poor shopkeepers constantly be returning money to me and then help me count my dinars when I accidentally overpay them, yet again. These positive human interactions are inspiring and uplifting.

Chapter 44

NUBIAN SEAMSTRESSES AND ASSUMPTIONS

I watch with thoughtful respect as a handful of women power their aged treadle sewing machines with their bare feet inside a one-room, makeshift factory made of dried mud where there is no electricity and no running water. Their homeland in the Nuba Mountains of Sudan is far, far away. They are hoping for a better life here, on the outskirts of Khartoum, about a mile after the tarmac road ends.

Two missionaries, whom I'd met through friends of friends, drove me in a borrowed Land Rover to this women's sewing cooperative which is managed by the missionaries' parent organization. All the proceeds from the sales of their wild-patterned, tie-dyed items go to these displaced Nubian women. They are making various and sundry items such as pants, aprons, tablecloths, bedspreads, and trivets. They also make an ingeniously designed, cylindrical bag with a small hole in one end, and out of which one easily pulls plastic grocery bags which one has stuffed inside for safe keeping and future use. The women tie-dye the fabric before they sew it into these useful items. I buy three pairs of bright, tie-dyed pants, and three tablecloths with matching napkins for myself. I buy other items as gifts for friends at home. My teaching salary is modest, and I have little money to spare, but spending my extra money here is the least I can do for these hard-working women. The prices are cheap, the quality is good, and the cause is worthwhile.

As we walk out of the one-room factory I take a few photographs of the shy Nubian children playing contentedly in the piping-hot desert sand outside. One is dressed in a faded, Flintstones T-shirt. They smile timidly as I snap a couple of pictures of them.

As we approach our Land Rover I am taken aback when one of the missionaries, seemingly in an attempt to make conversation, says to me, "No women are allowed inside the mosques in Sudan."

My response is immediate, and I tell her, "I know that your information is not correct because I was invited into the same mosque twice last year. Both times I prayed upstairs with the women while the men prayed downstairs. There were about one-hundred Muslim women upstairs with me."

The missionaries look astonished as I continue, "I asked the women if I could pray my prayers while they were praying their prayers, and they said, 'Yes.' So, I prayed my prayers inside their mosque, and it was a very powerful prayer experience for me."

I am telling the truth, but I have no idea if the missionaries believe me, or not. They look perplexed.

This is a good example of why every one of us constantly needs to check the source of the information on which we have built our beliefs, and then determine if what we are believing is fact or assumption. Sometimes we accept assumption as fact and, worse yet, sometimes we believe a downright lie as truth. Knowing this has been reason enough for me to learn from direct experience whenever possible, and this is the main reason I came to Khartoum. I wanted to learn about Muslim culture from first-hand experience, not hearsay.

We reach our vehicle. It's been baking in the desert sun for two hours. We open the car doors and windows to let the heat out. After a few minutes we take our seats. The missionary who is doing the driving assumes that the steering wheel has cooled off, and she grabs it. Instantaneously she recoils, lets out an anguished howl, and begins to cry. Within minutes she knows that she can't possibly drive because her hands hurt so terribly. The other missionary takes the driver's seat, and maneuvers us back home as her friend weeps in agony.

I learn later, from mutual friends, that she was diagnosed with second-degree burns on both of her hands. Her hands did heal, but it took several weeks of constant care. She was newly arrived to Sudan and did not understand the depth of respect the harsh desert sun deserves and demands.

The missionaries meant well. Their sewing cooperative is a noble project. It restores dignity to the displaced women, and provides them with a source of income in a part of the world where employment and wages are difficult to come by. The missionaries do have some lessons to learn, as we all do. Some of us have lessons that are easier, and some more brutal. The lesson is in the learning, and moving on the wiser.

Chapter 45

NUBIAN WRESTLERS
AND THEIR MOTHERS

On a blistering-hot Friday afternoon my friend, Norton, picked me up in his white Land Rover. Seated in the backseat were two of Norton's friends, visiting from England. Together, we set out in hopes of finding the elusive, outdoor, wrestling matches performed by men who are from the Nuba Mountain region of Sudan. I'd been told that foreigners are rarely, if ever, allowed inside the Nubian shanty towns. I was wondering if we'd feel welcome, or not, if we did managed to locate the shanty town that was hosting the wrestling matches that day.

To get there, Norton picked his way along mile after mile of dirt roads on the northeastern outskirts of Khartoum guided by a Nubian friend. (We'd stopped, en route, to pick up this friend at his dirt-floor house where his wife, with a genuine smile, had served us tea.) Without our guide we never would have found our way. The so-called roads were more like pathways that ran between mud huts inhabited by thousands of the poorest people imaginable, all of whom had relocated and settled in make-shift towns.

When we were deep inside Nubian territory, our Land Rover approached a crowd of teen-age boys and young men. They parted as we drew near. Our friend and guide caught the gist of their conversation and explained to us that a local boy had been caught for stealing. It was clear to me that he would never steal again. His lifeless body lay in a heap in the dry, desert sand. He'd been pummeled for the final time. As I averted my eyes from his motionless corpse, I thought, Stealing cannot be tolerated because life and death hang in the balance when each possession is critical to one's survival. Here the people's law must prevail because there is no money to hire and pay for official police.

Following in a vehicle behind ours was an emissary from the opposite end of the materialistic spectrum, a Saudi Arabian embassy official. He, his two kids, and a no-nonsense bodyguard were decked out in super-clean white very starched-and-polished, ankle-length, cotton gowns with hefty, gold cufflinks at the wrists, and red-and-white headdresses with black-leather headbands. The Saudis had received their invitation through Norton to come along on today's outing.

There were about two hundred Nubians in attendance that day, ninety percent of whom were men who had gathered in a large circle to watch the wrestling matches which took place in the center of the circle. My group consisted of Norton and his two English friends, the two adult Saudis, the two Saudi kids, and me. We were quite an attraction. Many of the Nubians looked at us with curiosity while we watched the wrestlers.

Each wrestling match lasted an average of two minutes. The contestants wrestled under the burning sun, in the hot desert sand, fair and square, man to man, bare chest to bare chest. Sweating, grunting, and groaning, the most excellent athlete won while the crowd cheered and yelled.

There was a charismatic, smiling, wiry chieftain of the wrestlers with a magnetic presence. He wore baggy, very faded, navy-blue sweatpants, and a bright-blue tam made of wool--and it had to have been at least 130 degrees that day--with plastic beads in a multitude of colors sewn all over it. He had a tail made of a broomstick affixed to his derriere, with bottle tops dangling and jangling off the end of it. While he danced and wove his way in, out, and around the wrestlers he switched and swayed his tail which made a wonderfully noisy, rattling-chattering sound.

And there were cheerleaders! They were anything but spring chickens, and were dressed in the most outrageously creative and garish getups you could imagine, or not imagine is more like it. One of the cheerleaders was dressed in a second-hand, 1950s bridesmaid dress made of daffodil-yellow and fuchsia-pink taffeta with ladies' slips in various colors, all with torn lace, worn over (not under!) her dress. Another of the cheerleaders flaunted a shoulder-length, homemade wig on her head fashioned out of neon-red yarn with doodads dangling off the sides. Yet another cheerleader wore several second-hand tops; the most conspicuous one had extra-puffy, elbow-length sleeves with a pattern of white polka-dots the size of fifty-cent pieces, and on the bottom she was wearing several plaid skirts, one on top of the other, each made from a different Scottish tartan. All of these gals carried, and waved, pom-poms made of something resembling tails from real horses. While dancing in rhythm, and chanting in unison, the cheerleaders strutted their stuff and stomped up a storm as they formed a circle around the men.

I asked Norton for a translation of the women's songs. He told me they were chanting, "Our side is winning. Our men are the strongest." Then he told me, "The cheerleaders are the mothers of the wrestlers." and this is where the wrestling match got mighty interesting and entertaining.

Whenever one of the wrestlers was getting too badly beaten by an opponent, his decked-out mother would jump on the opponent and seriously beat the crap out of that guy until a group of men pulled her off the guy she was pummeling. I couldn't help but fantasize and transport that scene to a wrestling ring in the U. S. Imagine decked-out and gussied-up, dancing, singing and strutting mothers of our wrestlers jumping into the ring every time they believed their sons were getting whooped too badly, and beating that opponent until the referees pulled her off. What a show!

Since going to the Nubian wrestling matches, I've talked to envious Westerners in Khartoum who have tried and tried, but never succeeded in seeing these elusive wrestling matches. I feel fortunate to have witnessed a lively, traditional event of a displaced people with a vibrant culture.

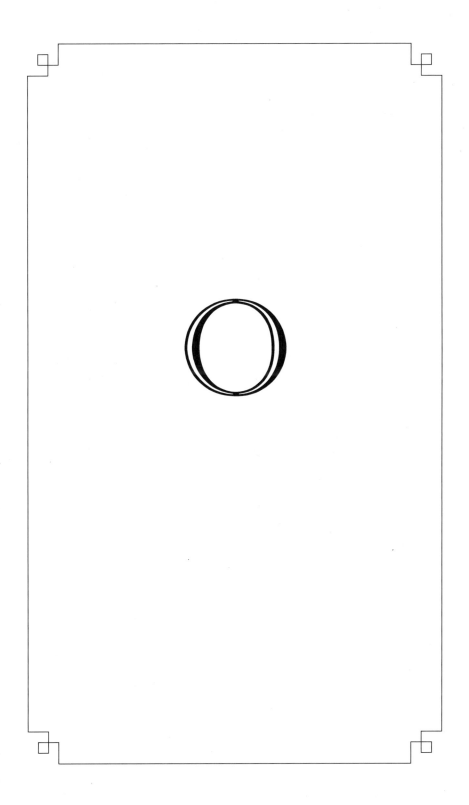

Chapter 46

ON SUDANESE TIME
AND INSHAA ALLAH

Vivaldi's soothing concertos serenade me from my CD player as I wait for Ashraf. He was supposed to have picked me up thirty minutes ago, and take me to his art studio to see his most recent watercolor paintings. Will he show up sometime soon? I don't know. Will he show up at all? Maybe. Most likely he will show up, he usually does, but not always.

Ashraf is a good friend and I have established an excellent, cross-cultural understanding about time with him. After we set a date and time for him to pick me up, I always ask, "Is that Sudanese time, or United States time?" which makes us laugh together, and then we establish which time system I should expect. He and I confirmed that today's get together is on "Sudanese time" which means that he will be relaxed about time today, and he might not show up at all. So I take it easy, listen to Vivaldi, and write this piece about time while I'm waiting. I'm wearing a comfy caftan. My street clothes are laid out and ready for me to put on should today's plan materialize.

Shortly after I arrived in Khartoum I realized that the Sudanese live according to a very different relationship to time compared to my cultural conception of time. I decided to adapt to the Sudanese way. My other choice would have been to slap my cultural expectations on top of the Sudanese. I didn't want to do that because that would have led to frustration upon frustration for me as well as for them, and it surely wouldn't have changed their behavior. This has necessitated that I temporarily relinquish my culture's habit of concrete, scheduled, start times and end times. The Sudanese have an inherent sense of when to begin and when to end whatever it is they are doing, and this has nothing to do with a ticking clock. Simply stated: time is not timed in Sudan.

Along with time existing within the context of natural flow, every get-together and event unfolds within the context of "God willing." I learned about "God willing" not long after I arrived when I asked a European-born friend, who has lived here for thirty years, about the phenomena of late arrivals, no-shows, events starting late, and called-off events in Khartoum. She answered me, saying, "That happens here. Whenever anyone Sudanese makes a date with you they spell out the specifics, and then they always add, 'inshaa Allah,' which means, God willing."

The attitude embodied in "God willing" would boggle the mind of every event planner, as well as most citizens, in the U.S. To make my point, I'll tell you a true story.

This story began when Islam, a Sudanese acquaintance of mine, initiated the idea of a music concert and accompanying party to be held on the deck of my apartment, and I agreed to host it. At this party two musicians were to perform. One of them was a female folk singer. The other was a male musician who plays the guitar and violin, and sings folk songs. Both were Sudanese, well-known, well-loved, and well-respected. So the party was kind of a big deal. Islam then told me on several occasions that the folk singers' concert was going to happen on such and such an evening, but several hours before the party was to take place Islam called it off. This phenomenon is typical along with the inshaa Allah state of mind in Khartoum. Before any event materializes there seem to be at least two called off and failed attempts at having that same event.

When the for-real folk singers' party was materializing, I didn't know until a couple of hours before it actually happened that it really was going to happen for sure. Since I don't have a telephone, and all phones are few and far between in Khartoum, I told as many people as possible by word of mouth about the party. Then I had to hope the word would somehow spread.

Thirty minutes before that party began, all I had in my cupboard was one case of Pepsi, and I was sweating it. I was not in a relaxed inshaa Allah mood at all. Instead, I was worried that I would fail in my role as hostess because I had nothing to feed my guests, very little for them to drink, and scarce few chairs for people to sit on. At that point in time I was new to Khartoum. I didn't know where to buy party food, and even if I had figured out where to get food for this party, I wouldn't have wanted to purchase it in advance because I wouldn't have wanted it to go to waste if the party was postponed again.

Lo and behold, my forty-five guests arrived more or less on time, and somehow they knew they were to bring food, drinks, and their own chairs. As the borrowed chairs were being arranged and the food was being laid out, I stood on the sidelines watching, and feeling astonished and extremely thankful that a force much greater than I was at work and willing this party to happen. Within minutes my dining-room table was overflowing with all kinds of cookies including butter cookies dusted with powdered sugar or decorated with multicolored sprinkles, freshly-made popcorn, baklava, and homemade cakes. The hit of the evening was a multilayered, white cake infused with fresh pineapple juice and sprinkled with freshly grated coconut. A giant pot of cold, crimson-red hibiscus tea was set down on the table, ready to be ladled. Pepsi was hauled into my apartment by the case loads. I could hardly believe my eyes. I had no idea how that party materialized until I reminded myself that it happened inshaa Allah.

From 6 p.m. until midnight, my Sudanese and American friends, and friends of friends, sat on my deck and enjoyed the folk music on a delightfully warm evening. During the breaks everyone chatted with each other, and devoured the food and drinks. All the guests left the party saying, "This was a really good party!" and they continued to tell me for weeks to come, "That was a great party!"

An interesting sideshow happened that evening. As the sound equipment was being carried up the outside stairs to my apartment, evidently word spread on the street, literally, that a party was afoot on my deck. All of the poor workers in the neighborhood, people such as off-duty gate guards and household employees, gathered outside the little shop across the street. They listened to the concert while standing to the side of the dirt road and they, too, clapped with enthusiasm when the music ended and the party was over. When I heard their applause, I looked down at the street from my third-floor deck to see what was going on. When this secondary audience of concertgoers saw me looking at them, they smiled and waved their hands in their appreciation and thanks. I smiled and waved back. I was glad I could provide an evening's entertainment to those in my neighborhood who were less fortunate, and for whom an inshaa Allah folk concert with esteemed musicians manifested free of charge.

Everyone, including the Sudanese, makes jokes about "Sudanese time." But, Sudanese time is one of the reasons why people are relaxed and happy. I look at Sudanese time as being in my favor. Here I am being offered a rare opportunity to slow down, so why not embrace it. With this attitude I have no frustration, no stress, and Sudanese doors open wide to me. When I return to Seattle I will, once again, plan ahead, arrive on time, and work from a well-thought-out To Do list because that's the way we get so much accomplished back home (and I do function this way in my teaching position at my school in Khartoum). Each way of organizing time has its trade offs.

Chapter 47

OVERNIGHT IN A POLLUTED CEMENT FACTORY

On our way home from an overland trip to the Red Sea, my friends and I spent the night in a dirty, cramped, guest house inside the walls of a huge cement factory in a city named Atbara. Why? Simply because there was no other place for travelers to spend the night in Atbara.

We'd arrived after dark, and we were hungry. Our guides and translator carried our bags inside, in a big hurry, and then left us in our suite of rooms--we each occupied a bedroom that opened onto a common living room--while they went on a shopping foray into Atbara for our dinner. Two hours later they returned with profuse apologies for taking so much time. They explained that there are no restaurants in Atbara, and all of the stores were closed for the evening. I don't know where they procured our dinner of sugary, canned, strawberry jam which we spread on locally-made, unsavory, white bread. We cut up the unpasteurized, tangy, feta cheese into small pieces and plunked it on top of the jam. While I ate my dinner I pictured Muhammad, our hired translator, knocking on the doors of Atbara houses, explaining his plight, and buying the items from the inhabitants of a house where there was extra food. And maybe that's what he did.

The next morning we were given a tour of the factory where we had spent the night. Thick, toxic smoke belched out of the factory's smoke stack. The manager, talking to us through our translator, explained, "He understand factory big pollution problem. He no have money for solve problem." The manager then appealed to us for help, asking us if we knew any organization from whom he could obtain the necessary funds to bring his factory up to quality environmental standards. I don't know if that cement factory was an environmental hazard or not, but from the look of that belching smoke I wouldn't be surprised if it was.

The factory workers wore a cross-cultural mishmash of traditional Sudanese garments along with functional attire from the West. Off-white turbans were tied around their heads. The turbans were lopsided and discolored as a result of the manual labor the men were doing. From the neck down they wore Western attire: grimy, drab-colored, loose-fitting pants and work shirts. Every one of the workers was eager to pose for me, and have his picture taken. I willingly complied.

I like the idea of having guest rooms in factories, with factory tours as part of an overnight package. The cement factory experience was much more interesting to me than spending the night in a motel or hotel in the U.S. This arrangement provided an opportunity to be educated about the workers and their environment, with a resulting and deserved appreciation for the work they do.

Chapter 48

OVERNIGHT IN THE DESERT AGAIN

I'm not new to overnights under the starry skies. I've spent a myriad of nights in my sleeping bag under the stars on beaches and in the lush, misty-green forest, and mountains of the Pacific Northwest as well as in the wilds of Idaho, Montana, Wyoming, British Columbia and Alaska. I spent a very different type of overnight in the stark, sandy, wind-blown Sahara desert of Sudan and, unlike the other overnights, getting out of town was a perilous adventure in itself.

On a Thursday in February, after school was over for the week, nine of us gathered at the home of a teacher from our school. As we clambered into the large Land Cruiser, I headed for the back seat, but everyone pushed me to the front passenger seat, saying, "You're riding in the passenger seat. We know you can handle it."

What my friends were referring to was a serious matter because Sudan is a police state. Everyone needs government-sanctioned travel permits to go anywhere in Sudan, including entering or exiting Khartoum. None of us had heard of anyone trying to leave Khartoum without the official paper work. Thus, we did not know what fate would be waiting for us at the checkpoints and roadblocks. One thing we knew for sure was that if we had trouble it would be big trouble. Big, difficult trouble.

I felt anxious as we headed north on the two-lane tarmac road. We all had cabin fever and we simply wanted to get out of town, and go into the desert on an overnight. Our intention was innocent, and it sounded relatively easy when we came up with the idea a few weeks ago. Now I was having second thoughts.

As we approached the roadblock, we slowed down to about one mile an hour in an attempt to not cause any alarm. My outward appearance was confident, but my mouth was dry as I nervously fingered my passport in the right breast pocket of my light-blue work shirt. If these soldiers detained us, I hoped that my U.S. passport was worth some bargaining power.

As our vehicle inched closer, I eyed the roadblock manned by soldiers with their rifles and machine guns. I began to think that we'd made a big mistake. I figured that our only hope would be for those Sudanese soldiers to somehow be convinced of our innocence and show their human side to us. My mind flashed on two experiences I'd had when soldiers had revealed a soft side to me.

One experience happened when I was living in Bogotá, Colombia, and there was a state of siege. Soldiers had been ordered to shoot and kill civilians on any street in Bogotá, but my friend and I were young, confident, impetuous nineteen-year-olds. After five days of being cooped up, she and I threw all notion of risk to the wind as we walked out of our apartment building. My honey-blonde, hip-length hair blew lazily in the breeze as she and I sauntered down our neighborhood street in mini-skirts. Young, handsome soldiers emerged from their armored tanks, and talked and flirted with us for a half-hour, or so, while they casually smoked their cigarettes. They needed relief from boring confinement as much as we did.

The other incident happened at a night-time curfew roadblock in Jerusalem when my Jewish friends and I were returning from an all-day romp and picnic. The Arab friend in our car should have been arrested, then and there, because he was out after dark, but the soldiers allowed us to enter the city without apprehending him.

However, one cannot be assured of a show of soldierly humanity, especially in a police state and in times of war. Both of these were the case in Sudan.

Our Land Cruiser stopped at the roadblock. I took my hand out of my breast pocket, and rolled down the window. One soldier approached us warily. He walked towards the passenger seat in which I was sitting. A dozen soldiers stood several meters behind him, all of them pointed their rifles at us. We all called out the Sudanese greeting, "Al salaam aleikum," as the lead soldier peered suspiciously into our vehicle from a distance of about one meter.

The soldier's wary eyes travelled over each occupant, and then to the Land Cruiser itself. In that instant I felt incredibly relieved that we were in an official Red Cross vehicle. Our driver and friend Margarite was a Red Cross employee, all of whom were given free use of company vehicles every weekend. But, I knew her bosses had not intended for their staffers to utilize the vehicles to sneak out of town illegally.

After studying the huge red cross painted across the hood of our vehicle, the soldier smiled a welcoming smile, and said a confident, "Marhaba!" and he waved us through the roadblock. "Marhaba" is the Sudanese version of "welcome," and the soldier had said it with all sincerity.

As we sped away from the checkpoint, I felt simultaneously guilty and elated. Guilty because the soldier thought we were on official Red Cross business and we'd used this vehicle to manipulate his understanding of our intentions, and elated that we'd successfully escaped from the bondage of Khartoum. I whispered several prayers of thanks, particularly to the Red Cross and its contributors.

Someone in the back seat said, "That was easy, thank God!" and all of us erupted in joy-filled whoops. It was as if we'd made a successful jail break.

We drove north for about forty-five minutes. Then Christie, a very skinny, dark-skinned, thirty-year-old Sudanese woman who wore her hair in scores of tiny braids drawn into a pony-tail, said in a thick Sudanese accent, "Turn left here."

Hmmm, I thought to myself, I wonder where we're going because we are in the middle of absolute nowhere, and there's nothing but desert stretching out on all sides of us.

Pint-sized Margarite swerved to the left and crossed over the oncoming traffic lane, but that didn't matter because we hadn't passed any oncoming traffic on our entire trip, and there were no other vehicles in sight. As she turned off the tarmac road, she crammed that Cruiser into four-wheel drive and began maneuvering through the deep sand with the determination of a seasoned truck driver. We fishtailed in and out of sand drifts, and we cruised up and over sand dunes. Our Land Cruiser rode up and over the desert's drifts and dunes like a luxury liner riding the ocean waves and I thought, Land Cruiser is the perfect name for this mighty-fine vehicle.

Margarite started talking about Sahara desert snakes. I loathe snakes, and my spine tingled with anxiety as she said, "The people in my office tell me that the snakes here are about seven inches long, and they're deadly. They burrow a few inches under the sand so you can't see them, can't see them until it's too late." That was news to me. I hoped I wouldn't regret coming on this overnight outing.

Fifteen minutes later we pulled up next to a jebel. Jebel is the Arabic word for hill or mountain, and this particular jebel was what I'd call a mountainous pile of boulders. Christie said, "This is our jebel. This is our destination." I will never understand how Christie knew how to navigate us there because there were no landmarks discernible to me, and it was impossible to see the jebel when we turned off the main road because of the surrounding sand dunes. This was yet another secret held by the desert and its native dwellers.

An hour later, a full moon was rising into a cloudless sky as we gathered around our campfire and ate a delectable dinner. Our first course was a salad of juicy, red tomatoes and fresh feta cheese. We sopped up the drippings with bread which was the Sudanese version of a baguette. It's similar to a foot-long U.S. hot dog bun, and is the mainstay of the Sudanese diet. Our entrées were chicken marinated in fresh lime juice and garlic, and kofta which is a tasty and traditional Sudanese food made of ground beef, bread, and spices all rolled up into little sausages and meatballs, and baked in the oven. For dessert we savored homemade peanut butter and chocolate chip cookies. They tasted really special because the chocolate chips were hand-carried from the U. S. to Khartoum. There was very little, if any, chocolate of any kind available in Khartoum, and chocolate chips could not be found anywhere. We appreciated the cookies as a rare treat. We all sat close to our campfire, talking and laughing for a few hours after dinner.

After everyone went to bed, I slipped into my full-length, polypro long johns, a thick, polar-fleece coat, and extra-warm sweat pants. I pulled my woolly, gray, watchman's cap onto my head and as close to my eyes as possible for protection from the wind that was blasting sand into my face and eyes, and up my nose. Then I roamed around the desert for hours. It's hard to put my experience into words, but I was certain I had walked that dry, sandy land many times before. Somehow, this foreign landscape felt very familiar. As I wandered near the jebel in the soft sand, my moon-lit shadow beside me, I offered prayers of thanks and exaltation. I felt as if I were being held in the palm of God, one of whose names is Allah.

Everyone else was asleep when I bedded down. I nestled into my sleeping bag which I'd placed next to the fading embers in our fire pit, but I couldn't sleep. How could I sleep when it was so beautiful? I sat up and looked, and looked at the rich, stark beauty surrounding me. I turned my head and eyes from side to side, again and again, drinking in the magnificence of the desert lit by a full moon. Not far from me were heaps of rocks casting strange, shadowy shapes onto the desert floor in the full-moon night. Small mountains made of huge boulders loomed in the distance.

The moon looked like a gigantic, sky peach as it set below the horizon and I finally felt ready to sleep. I lay on my back, on the hard desert sand, and prayed that neither the cold-blooded viper snakes nor the scorpions would want to snuggle against, and cause harm to, my warm body. I rolled onto my left side, and was blasted by sand blowing into my nostrils and up my nose. I rolled onto my right side, blew the sand out of my nose as best I could, and fell asleep. A few hours later, I was awakened by the brilliance of a shimmering, bright orange, rising sun.

As we broke camp that morning, packing our brightly colored, synthetic-fabric sleeping bags and tents, we were watched by a local shepherd boy who had climbed partway up the jebel and, keeping a respectful distance of about sixty meters, watched us from his perch on an outcropping of rocks. How alien we must have looked with our white skin, and our camping gear made of artificially bright, man-made materials.

I strolled across the sand, and climbed the rocks to the shepherd boy's perch. Believing that cookies are ambassadors of goodwill in any culture, I smiled and extended my hand in which I held an unopened packet of Sudanese-made cookies. After studying both me and the cookies for a couple of unhurried, quiet minutes, he stretched out his arm and hand, and accepted the cookies with a reserved smile.

As I walked back to join my friends, I wondered how long it would be before I returned to spend a night, or longer, in this harsh, rich, familiar desert.

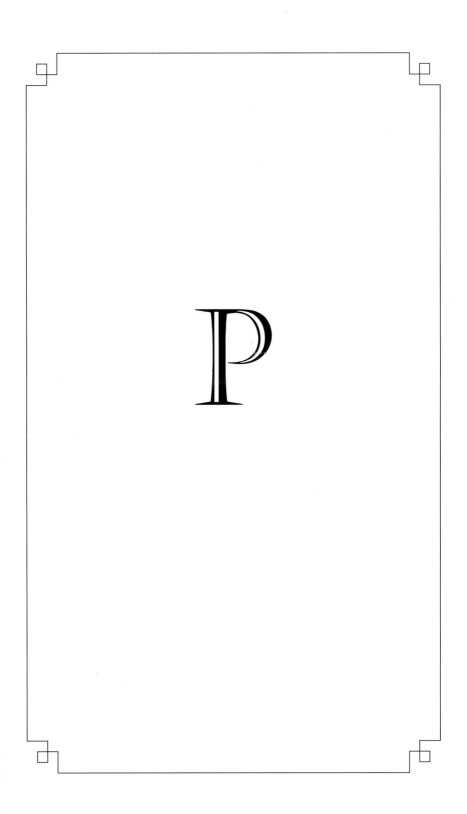

Chapter 49

PIGEON-PECKED BUFFET

When I saw pigeons pecking at the food that would be served on our plates, I knit my brow in disgust. Inside my head I yelled at myself, What are you doing here?! You're risking your life. You could get a deadly pigeon-carried disease from this food. You need to get out of here!

It was a sunny afternoon. I'd gone with six other teachers, a couple of Sudanese friends, and a Brit to eat homemade Indian food in a so-called restaurant. I referred to it as "so-called" because it was located inside a private house where restaurant patrons ate family style, literally, with the proprietress' husband and their three kids at the same, small, dining room table. The little, mud-brick, five-room home was surrounded by a red-brick wall with an iron entry gate painted sky-blue. The proprietress had no telephone. So a patron needed to go in person the day before wanting to eat a meal, make an in-person reservation, and then show up the following day for the vegetarian Indian food. On the bumpy, one-lane, dirt street on which the house was located, it was of paramount importance to hug the right side of the road because there was a long, ten-foot ditch on the left side of the road.

The meal was served buffet-style on a simple, wooden, dining room table from which you had a view of the inner, open-air courtyard where her garbanzo beans were drying outside on the ground in the hot sun. Wild pigeons pecked vigorously at the beans. When I saw those pigeons pecking at the garbanzos, that's when my mind began to get carried away, and I fretted about what type of disease I was going to get from the food. I quickly told that screechy voice inside my head to, Pipe down and have a good time! And a good time I did have as I ate my fill of dish after dish of tasty food with all kinds of spicy condiments and fresh, creamy, white yogurt on the side. My friends and I ate until we were so stuffed we couldn't possibly eat any more. Other than the garbanzos and yogurt, I had no idea what I was eating. I can assure you that it was all delicious; and it cost only 4,000 Sudanese dinars per person which is equivalent to more or less $2.25 in U.S. dollars.

There you have it, a true story about an authentic, dirt-cheap, Indian buffet in Khartoum. No, I didn't get sick afterwards, and it was great fun, truly. Therefore, you can cautiously conclude that when traveling or living in an exotic land, it can be worthwhile to turn a blind eye to pecking pigeons.

Chapter 50

POLICE STATE AND CHECKPOINTS

Sudan is a police state. This means that everyone is in twenty-four-hour lockup in the city in which they reside. No one can enter or exit any Sudanese city without a stack of official documents. Everyone has to reapply for these documents every single time he or she goes in or out of Khartoum, or in or out of any city in Sudan. The documents have to be sanctioned, and stamped, by an assortment of officials at various government offices. This is time-consuming, to say the least. The fact that there is only one road leading in, and out, of each city makes it easy for the military to check all comings and goings. Roadblocks and checkpoints manned by soldiers with plenty of guns and ammunition are on all roads and highways.

Within Khartoum there are a few daytime checkpoints, and many after-dark curfew checkpoints. If you're a foreigner with white skin, you don't need paperwork to pass through these checkpoints. The soldiers will give both you and the inside of your vehicle a cursory, and usually friendly, once-over and then they wave you on. But only if you slow down. And stop. A French woman did not slow down and stop. She got shot. She was driving her car, with four passengers inside, too fast and too close to the road that leads to the presidential palace, and bang! The soldiers fired at her car. She was shot in the thigh and taken to a local hospital. This can be a death sentence in itself because all hospitals here are short on both medicine and doctors. Several days later, I heard via the expatriate grapevine, that the woman's wound was healing. However, my tenth-grade students told me that she was dead, which wasn't true. This proved to be a good case in point about rumors in Khartoum where the rumor mill runs rampant. One needs to confirm the authenticity of all information obtained by word of mouth. The French woman did live to tell her tale, but it was a significant reminder to be vigilant about one's driving practices in and around Khartoum's checkpoints.

It's serious business at the entry and exit points to all cities, as well as at the highway checkpoints and roadblocks. They are manned by plenty of military personnel armed with an abundance of artillery. At every highway checkpoint there's a large platoon of soldiers working and living around the clock. When not standing at attention, they sit or sleep on the traditional Sudanese bed called an angareb. An angareb is a saggy, single bed with four bedsteads made of hand-split chunks of wood strung together with a web of macramé knots made of nylon rope. A slim mattress is placed on top of the macramé webbing. The mattress is always made of locally-grown cotton. The soldiers take shelter from the intense sun, as well as sleep, inside of beige cotton tents with pointed roofs and drooping sides. Doesn't seem like a rewarding place to work and live.

We stopped at many police checkpoints where our papers were examined, scrutinized, and reexamined again and again during our seven-day spring-break trip to the Red Sea. Soldiers, dressed in camouflage gear, manned their posts with rifles and kept machine guns pointed at us while others checked all of our necessary travel documents. Our guide and translator, Muhammad, kept the required papers neatly arranged in a portfolio which he held on his lap at all times for easy access. The stack of papers was an inch thick. We'd wait patiently while they inspected the documents. We weren't about to bolt. If we did, we would have been riddled with bullets. Also, the soldiers always radio ahead with your description alerting the next roadblock to be expecting you. There's no escaping them.

Travelling south from Khartoum every vehicle has to stop and show identification papers at checkpoints approximately every eight miles. The further south you travel, the tighter the security and the more checkpoints you have to pass through. This is because of the civil war that has raged for years in the south of Sudan. It's easier to travel north because there isn't a war in the north, and one encounters checkpoints only about every thirty miles. North and south, by the way, are basically the only two directions you can travel by road here. I don't recommend travelling off-road for long unless you're riding on a camel led by locals, and that would be sure to present its own set of challenges.

The roadblocks and checkpoints are unnerving at times, but I haven't heard of anyone who didn't survive them which is at least something of a consolation.

Chapter 51

PRAY TO ALLAH BUT TIE YOUR CAMEL FIRST

"Pray to Allah but tie your camel first" is a well-known expression in the Arab world. This saying is more or less the same as "God helps those who help themselves" but I really like the addition of the image of the camel to add some humor and spice.

To make this expression come alive, I'll give a couple of examples of putting it into practice.

An excellent case in point regarding "tie your camel first" is the practice of carrying extra water and gas in your vehicle in case you get lost during a desert crossing. Our driver did exactly this when we made a ten-hour crossing through the Sahara desert on our way back to Khartoum from a trip to the Red Sea. We did get frightfully lost on that trip, and it was reassuring to know that we had extra water and gas (even though it was a finite amount). As for prayer, I was praying like mad that we would find our way that day, and I gave thanks to God when we reached our destination. I can't vouch for our guide, drivers, navigators and translator, but I'm laying odds that they were praying, too.

In the introduction to this book I explain how preparation and prayer landed me in Sudan. Prior to receiving the job offer to teach in Khartoum, I spent considerable time and thought tying my camel, so to speak. In other words, I rewrote and updated my résumé with care, and then networked with countless people over many weeks. Along with that groundwork, I prayed for the job that was in my highest good, the highest good of all those whose lives I would touch, and in the highest good of all those whose lives would touch mine. When my phone rang and my future boss (whom I'd never met) offered me a teaching position in Khartoum, I was beyond surprised. I'd been expecting to find a job somewhere in the Pacific Northwest, maybe as far away from Seattle as Coos Bay, Oregon. Instead, I was offered a job in Sudan. This was a good reminder that sincere preparation and prayer is not for the faint of heart because one must be willing to accept and trust the wisdom of a higher intelligence, which can be very different from one's surface desires.

Thinking "Pray to Allah but tie your camel first" will remind you to make your preparations with care because God can't tie your camel for you, and then trust as you pray. Saying "Pray to Allah but tie your camel first" can inject humor into just about any situation because, to a Western mind, the image of a camel is almost certain to bring a smile and a chuckle.

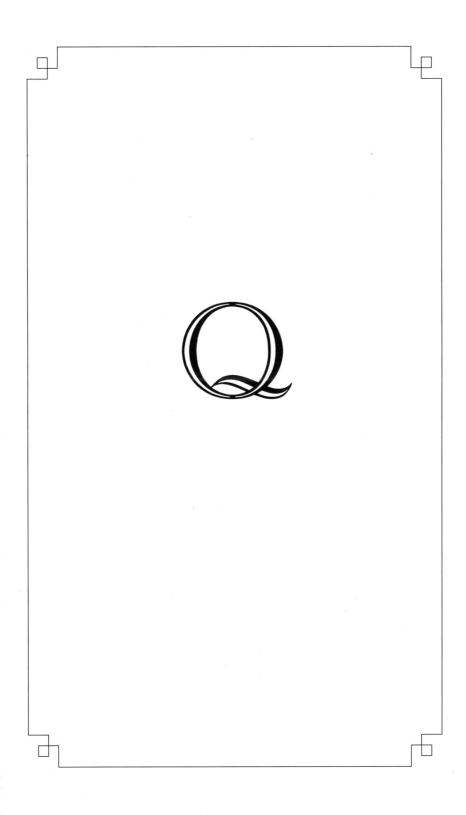

Chapter 52

QUARRY CAVE AND A TINY, TIMELESS TRAVELER

Rocks were quarried for the pyramids at Meroe 2,500 years ago from a cave that continues to be accessible today. One simply needs to tromp a half mile across the desert from the pyramids, and climb a rocky hill to gain entrance to the cave. But beware! Black bats, hundreds of them, will swoop toward and around you in droves.

Immediately after entering the cave, five of the people in my group took a quick exit because they couldn't stand the bats buzzing the tops of their heads. Four of us stayed, and walked through the cave which was lit by several narrow natural openings to the bright sunlight. At the far end of the cave we crouched down to pass through a narrow opening, and we stood outside on a rocky cliff looking at an expanse of desert. Nothing but flat desert stretched to the horizon in every direction.

The other three, wanting relief from the scorching sun, ducked back into the cave. I stood alone on the cliff. In the distance, about a quarter of a mile from me, was a tiny figure, a male child of about seven years old dressed in a traditional, white jalabeya and white cap. Alone and unhurried, he walked along the searing-hot floor of the desert, barefoot. I could see no other signs of civilization, and I wondered where he'd come from and where he was going.

Then, he reached his little arms ever so slowly toward the sky. With his arms raised in exaltation, he began twirling in long, slow circles as he moved westward. He was so calm, so free, so unencumbered. As I watched him, I wondered what my mental, emotional, and spiritual life would be like had I grown up walking alone in that expansive desert in my little jalabeya, not influenced by the complex ways of modern, city life filled with compulsions to do, do, do and desires to acquire, acquire, acquire. Twenty minutes later he was continuing to move in wonderfully relaxed circles, but I felt absolutely wilted and I tucked back into the cool cave for relief.

As the bats buzzed the top of my head, I wondered if feeling horribly hot is really a state of mind. Is it possible to live in this scorching heat and choose not to suffer from it? The child, in his state of exaltation, was an authentic demonstration of what sages throughout time have attempted to teach us: live fully in this present moment accepting life as it is.

Chapter 53

QUIET PICNIC

When Sudanese friends invited me to ". . . go to a picnic . . ." I gladly accepted the invitation. I didn't have the slightest idea what to expect of a Sudanese picnic, but I'm always keen on spending time with locals doing local things. I was quite sure that even though they'd said the word "picnic" the event would not be anything like ours at home when we pack special foods, and then go somewhere outdoors to enjoy a natural setting as we eat. Since I like surprises, I decided it would be fun to keep myself in suspense. So, I asked no questions, and I was careful not to make up scenarios in my mind, positive or negative. Having no expectations would allow the mystery to unfold naturally, just as it was meant to be.

The day of the picnic arrived. After about a half hour of driving, Ashraf parked his car in a dirt parking area. His friends and I got out of the car, walked around a bend in a path, and I could hardly believe what I saw up ahead, nothing but dense green foliage. I wondered, Are we in the Sahara desert or have we been transported?

We entered the fertile green area through a large, wrought-iron gate, and then strolled leisurely through tranquil, lush gardens brimming with colorful roses, thick bamboo, many shrubs, and enormous, green, leafy trees filled with wild song birds singing welcoming songs. It was as if I'd been carried off to paradise.

Filled with awe, I asked, "Where are we?"

My friends were taking great pleasure in the incredulous expression on my face, and they chuckled as they answered, "We are at a farm on the banks of the Nile River owned by friends of ours."

I said softly, "Oh, now it makes sense."

The farm was a testimony to the fact that, standing on the banks of the Nile, you'd never know you're in the middle of an enormous country filled with desert sand.

Lunch was a luscious meal of traditional Sudanese food. For our entrée we ate savory kebobs. Our kebobs consisted of skewers filled with fresh, white onions, green peppers, and chunks of succulent beef fillet marinated in unusual and tasty spices and barbequed until tender. We were also served pocket bread, cucumber and tomato salad, baba ganoush, and traditional foul made from gently cooked fava beans that had been mashed with exotic spices. I helped myself to a healthy amount of very-spicy hot sauce which I drizzled over my feast.

We sat in comfy lawn chairs under the shade of tall, bushy, green trees and ate our picnic lunch while Michael Jackson's music blared in the background. Listening to the song birds was more enjoyable to me than the rock music. It seemed to be the opposite for the Sudanese people. They're accustomed to hearing the birds singing, and Michael Jackson's music was exotic to them.

Not much from Western culture enters Sudan. For example, I wasn't allowed to bring any magazines, much less music, when I entered this country. I did sneak in three Smithsonian magazines which I kept on the coffee table in my living room, and which my Sudanese guests pored over with unwavering attention. I also packed a few CDs by musicians such as Afro Celt Sound System as well as the Wicked Celts (who are personal friends of mine) and which my Sudanese friends listened to with wonder and appreciation.

The picnic was really different from our parties because no one was saying much, but everyone looked comfortable and content. Since I wasn't expected to talk, I took the opportunity to relax. I ate slowly, thoroughly enjoying my picnic food, as my eyes feasted on the surrounding greenery which was gorgeous to me because all I usually see here is endless desert.

As usual, I was the only person with white skin at the party, and I felt very welcome. I always feel welcome at Sudanese gatherings. I appreciate the fact that the Sudanese relate to people based on their character rather than judging them according to the color of their skin or their country of origin.

After we finished eating, everyone sat for quite awhile not saying much of anything to anyone. Then it was time to leave. We strolled through the garden, got into the car, and went home.

Coming from my cultural background it was, at first, a mystery to me why people would gather together at a picnic to eat and sit quietly. As the afternoon progressed it was apparent that all the guests were quite content, and that's what's important. As a result of going to that quiet picnic, I decided it's pleasurable to not feel any obligation to talk at a party and be "on," so to speak. Much to my surprise it was a welcome relief, and thus another lesson learned in the lush desert. When I get back home, I've decided to host a quiet picnic at my house. Maybe I can start a new, pleasurable, relaxed tradition in picnicking.

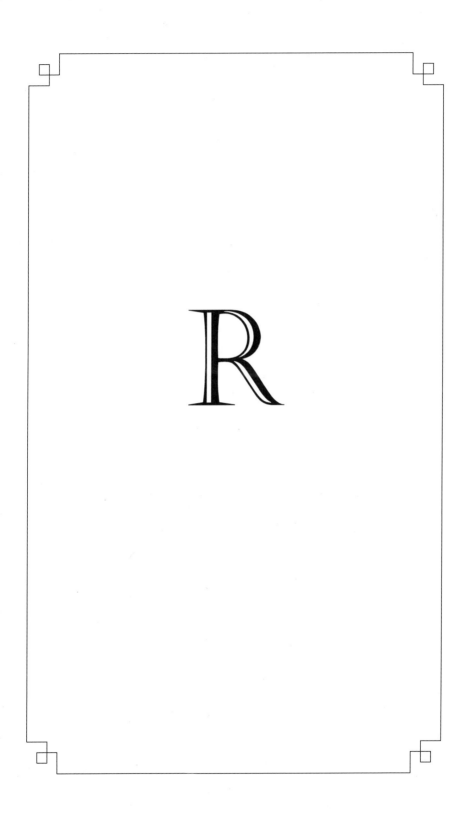

R

Chapter 54

RAMADAN KINDNESS

Kindnesses were extended to me in surprising ways during Ramadan. For example, one afternoon when I arrived at my home after a long day of work, my gate guard handed me a plate of homemade cookies and candies with the following note written in broken English:

Dear ANILA

I hope you are well and everything is going OK with you.

I came last week and today at afternoon but I didn't met you, so I hope you are well.

Now I came with Hassan my friend to send you this sweets as a gift from Hassan's mother. She would like to give you sweets. And we all hope you will like it very much.

I'll come in Tuesday at 6:00 p.m. I hope you will be home at that time, if you have anything else please call me at home in evening everyday between 6 up to 10.00 pm

See you soon,
ASHRAF
"TUMSAH"

Ashraf was my Arabic teacher. At the bottom of the note he wrote his phone number, and sketched a car with a crocodile lying on top of the car. This is because, as Ashraf once explained to me, when he was a small child his cousins gave him the nickname Tumsah. A tumsah is a crocodile, and when Ashraf was a little boy he always slept on his back with his mouth open and, therefore, he looked like a crocodile.

Along with the fun drawing, what touched my heart was that I had never met Hassan's mother. Yet, she made sweets for me. I can't tell you how much her thoughtfulness meant to me. This would be like you or me baking, and giving, a plate of our finest, handcrafted and decorated Christmas cookies and candies to a Muslim we had never met, simply as a gesture to make that person feel at home in our country during a meaningful time of the year.

The sweets were delicious and served as a good reminder that a plate of cookies and candies made with love forges friendships and extends goodwill in any culture.

Chapter 55

RESORT LIVING
AND TRAVELLING
THROUGH LIFE

Roads were nonexistent and there weren't any people to be seen as our Land Rover drove north out of Port Sudan on a sunny, spring morning. We followed the Red Sea along sand dunes inhabited by packs of wild camels. Our destination was a resort which was about thirty miles north of Port Sudan at a place named Arous, which means bride of the sea.

For three blissful days I roamed Arous's sun-scorched, white-sand, unpopulated beaches. Shells littered the beaches by the thousands, making it difficult to find my footing. There were more shells than sand, and I'm laying odds that all of our beaches looked like that once upon a time prior to being invaded by millions of modern-day shell snatchers. There was never another soul in sight except once when a nomad, who was way in the distance, spotted me and began walking toward me. A Muslim nomad would definitely have gotten the wrong idea about my intentions since I was all by myself, and clothed only in my bathing suit and a sarong. This was a far cry from being covered head to toe like a proper female Muslim. When the nomad spied me, I turned around and began walking back to the resort, very fast.

For three days I swam in warm, pristine, turquoise waters amongst a kaleidoscopic incarnation of Red Sea fish and coral, the colors of which defy human vocabulary. I swear that every imaginable underwater color, pattern, hue and texture exists in the Red Sea off of Arous in such a tantalizing combination it's enough to make a true believer out of you, if you weren't one already. The waters at Arous were the most pristine I've ever snorkeled in, and that includes the Caribbean, the waters off the Hawaiian Islands, and the Indian Ocean. Why are these Sudanese waters so pristine? Because Sudan doesn't have any modern-day industry to pollute and ravage the Red Sea.

The pleasures I experienced in the water and on the beaches were a far cry from my landlocked experiences.

Wild camel country surrounds Arous. An untamed camel sauntered past the front window of my cabin, and parked itself in the sand outside my cabin door during my first night in Arous. It sat there slurping, belching, crunching, and grumping all night long. Since I'm a light sleeper, that camel's noises made for a night of interrupted sleep. I spent more time awake than asleep. Shortly before dawn I gave up trying to get back to sleep. I got out of bed, pulled on a loose-fitting, three-quarter sleeve, white, cotton top and a pair of comfy, baggy, tie-dye cotton pants (which I'd bought from the Nubian seamstresses' cooperative in Khartoum). I grabbed my camera, stormed across my cabin, and pried open the sagging front door. There the camel sat, sprawled across the front steps, blocking my exit. I then did something which is entirely out of character for me, a U.S. city girl who did not grow up around animals, much less wild camels. I began to order that camel around; and what was even more strange, that camel did absolutely everything I demanded of it.

From the top of the decomposing steps to the cabin, I barked my orders, "Hey you! Camel! Get up. Now! I was awake almost all night long because of you! You messed with me and now it's your turn to do something for me. Get your butt off the ground. Get marching! We are going for a photo shoot. And you are going to do every single thing I tell you to do!"

That camel obeyed me. For the next hour, no matter what I told it to do, it did it. For example, I yelled, "I can't quite see the sunrise. You're blocking it a little. You need to back up two feet! Now!" And that undomesticated camel backed up two feet; no less, no more. I carried on, roaring an hour's worth of orders.

The upside is that I ended up with fabulous photographs of the sun rising in back of that camel. Within minutes after I bid that creature farewell, I was laughing out loud about the entire episode.

However, my rustic cabin was not a laughing matter. It was situated on white sand next to the gorgeous turquoise Red Sea, but that's the only thing it had going for it. Whatever the word "rustic" brings to your mind would not do justice to my cabin. For three nights I slept, or I should say tried to sleep, with a ceiling fan that didn't revolve, an air conditioner that worked only when the light was on making it almost impossible for me to sleep. Not only was the room filled with a glaring light at night, but the air conditioner was horribly noisy. However, I found it difficult to sleep when it was off because my cabin was sweltering. There were musty-smelling bed sheets, no bathroom towels, and only a few small squares of toilet paper. There was no mosquito net, and malaria-carrying mosquitoes shrieked in my ears all night long. I doused my body with citronella oil, along with insect repellent made from chemicals, but they bit me anyway. That necessitated visualizations and affirmations on my part that I would not get malaria. (I did not get malaria, thank God.)

But, wait. I'm not finished. There was only one light and that was in the form of a light bulb swinging from a frayed, electric cord in the middle of the room. The broken-down bed was listing to starboard. The front door locked, but not very well. There was a small window in the front of the cabin, but because it was stuck shut I couldn't get a cross-draft in that stuffy room. The back window was askew, and could be lifted up and opened by anyone at anytime; it was raised up constantly by our guide Muhammad. He, after stuffing yards of his ankle-length jalabeya between his legs, along with an extra-firm tuck into his crotch, would climb into my cabin through the open window space so he could get the rusty, broken toilet to flush. After completing this chivalrous act he would depart via the same open window. Entering and exiting through the window made much more sense than using the front door which sagged, and dragged, across the floor making it difficult to open and close. The back window slid right on up, so why not use it instead of the troublesome front door.

My five friends and I were fed three meals a day in the outdoor restaurant. I never had a clue what I was eating, other than the fish. The flavors were new to my taste buds. I didn't get sick from the food, and it was delicious. Thus, the food was a redeeming feature. The restaurant itself left something to be desired. It amounted to a cracked-cement outdoor patio with several falling-apart metal chairs and a couple of old, banged-up metal tables.

I got all this for the equivalent of $80.00 U.S. dollars a day. An overpriced eighty! Snorkel equipment was another $35.00 a day extra; fortunately I'd brought my own.

Would I return to Arous? Yes, I would. The snorkeling was superb, the food divine, and the beaches pristine. The resort itself was a relic from bygone days when travelers and vacationers were welcome in Sudan. Those days will return, and when tourism opens up again, I'm urging you to go. Go and be in the first wave to experience this unspoiled treasure. Who knows, maybe Arous will have been updated. Even if it hasn't been modernized, you could meet up with an intriguing, wild camel or a mystical chap from the local Hadendoa tribe named Abu Medino from whom you could learn a thing or two. (I share my memorable adventures with Abu in Chapter 1.)

When you travel in Sudan, or in any foreign country for that matter, my advice is: expect the upside to have a downside and vice versa, laugh really hard at least once a day, cultivate a welcoming heart, and have a mindset for understanding, respecting, accepting, and learning from those around you including wild camels. Be on the lookout for unexpected blessings because they will come to you, and keep the faith during the times when those blessings aren't coming because you never know what's around the next corner. Stay open to the wonder as well as to the responsibility that comes with the awareness of dwelling in an increasingly smaller world. Looking at it this way, resort life and travelling through Sudan is really no different than travelling through life.

Chapter 56

REST STOPS AND REFLECTIONS

Picture the rest stops along Interstate Highways in the United States. Easy to find, spacious, orderly, clean, wheelchair accessible, with functioning water faucets and toilets. They usually have enough room around the perimeter to stretch both your and your pet's legs, and are frequent enough to accommodate almost all people's needs no matter how young or old. Many have welcome centers, vending machines, picnic tables, and scenic views.

Sudanese rest stops are not at all like those in the U.S, and they are where we took our travel breaks on our roundtrip, overland adventure from Khartoum to the Red Sea. All of them are a variation on the same theme. The structures are made in the shape of a crude lean-to. Tree branches, which give support to the roofs, have been stuck into the desert sand. Roofs are made of thatched mats, and provide welcome, albeit temporary, relief from the sun. Walls are also made of thatched mats. There are miniature-size, scratched, metal tables and chairs that look as though they've endured generations of use, and there are stools of a similar description with seats made of remnants of woven rope.

Food and drink is for sale at the rest stops in Sudan; no restaurants exist in the Sahara desert so this is the only place to obtain sustenance. It is usually sold by a dark-skinned woman wearing the traditional tobe.

Each of these women is typically chubby--almost all Sudanese women are twenty to forty pounds overweight by U.S. standards--and she looks as if she is in her forties. She sits on a small, square stool while quietly making strong coffee and tea on a traditional stove which uses charcoal for fuel. Occasionally a middle-aged man in a jalabeya does the same job.

The most popular drink in Sudan is Pepsi. (The Sudanese pronounce it "bib-see" with the accent on bib, because there is no p sound in Arabic.) Pepsi and water are available at all the rest stops, and there are no other choices for beverages. Since water is the quickest and surest way for me to get violently sick with dysentery or die, I drink Pepsi.

The food is carried to a group of travelers on a single, large, round, gray, aluminum tray. Each item is placed on a separate plate on that metal tray, without any silverware. Everyone eats Sudanese-style, out of common dishes with their fingers. You partake of your meal by holding the fingers of your right hand together, and making a scoop out of your right hand. The entrée is always a sloppy mixture of thick pieces of white bread, similar in taste and texture to Wonder Bread, cut into chunks and dumped onto a large plate with a greasy meat sauce ladled over it. It tastes as bad as it sounds.

I wouldn't consider eating this slop in Khartoum, much less in the States. But there I was in the Sahara desert consuming it, and then washing the whole mess down with a Pepsi or two, or three, depending on how thirsty I was which, again, was unlike me because I drink about one soda a year at home. All the while I was shooing masses of large, black flies off the food, off my lips, out of my eyes, and off my body.

My European traveling companions and I were the main attraction at the rest stops because their skin was as white as mine, and their kids were towheads. We were always the only ones with white skin and light hair; everyone else had brown or black skin with African features.

The further away from Khartoum and the deeper into the desert we travelled, the fewer people there were at each rest stop, and the more desperate their circumstances seemed to be. Three days away from Khartoum, we stopped midmorning at a rest stop and were immediately surrounded by a bevy of dark-skinned, emaciated, older women begging for money. Each woman placed the first two fingers of her right hand together and pointed to her mouth, and then to the beat-up, dented, aluminum bowl she was carrying. Each had a gold ring pierced into the left side of her nose. (I had never before seen a pierced nose in Sudan.) Stripped of all modicum of dignity, they were dressed in tattered, Western-style dresses over which was draped a limp and faded tobe.

Just then, a jeep loaded with soldiers dressed in camouflage gear, sped toward the rest stop, and came to an abrupt halt about twenty yards from where I was sitting. From my lopsided chair, I watched several of the hapless, scrawny women slither over to the virile, cocky soldiers. They each unbuttoned their dresses, exposing their bare, shriveled breasts. I wanted to run to these women, ask them how much money they would receive for turning a trick, and give them an equal amount of money. But I stopped myself. Giving them money wouldn't have done a damn bit of good. I felt deep sadness because their only means of survival was begging, or prostitution.

As I witnessed the rest stop prostitutes, I reflected on my blessings. I felt incredibly thankful for my bachelor's and master's degrees from the university--albeit I did work my rear off studying, and paying for my tuition, but at least I had the choice--my teaching certificate, my U.S. passport, my freedom to make choices and to act on them, my mobility, my accumulation of world travel and real-life experiences, and all of my resulting knowledge and understandings. I felt ashamed that I had indulged in self-pity during my stay in Khartoum because sometimes I'm treated unkindly at school by my colleagues, and because my excellent Seattle friends live so far away. The injustice of the plight of these women and the immensity of my good fortune glared at me, and I bowed my head in gratitude.

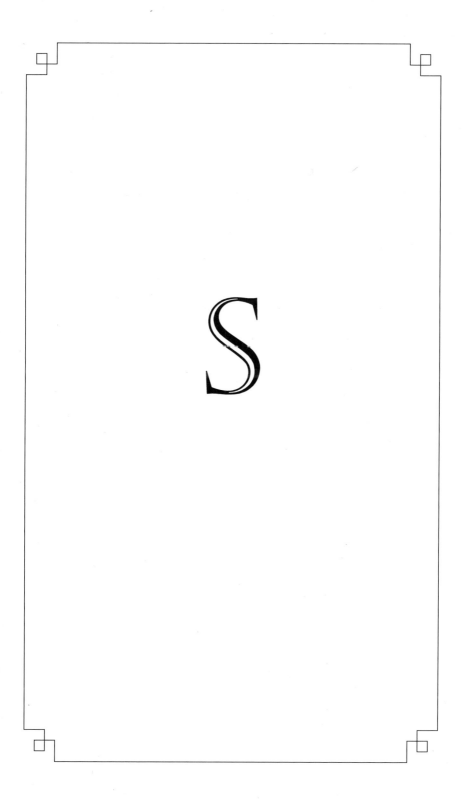

Chapter 57

SACRED CHRISTMAS GIFT FROM MUSLIMS

I was crying and sitting on the couch in my living room when I heard a knock on my front door. I sucked in a breath, made myself stop crying, brushed the tears from my cheeks, and blew my nose. I walked to my front door, and found my Arabic teacher and good friend, Ashraf. He had arrived unexpectedly. Standing rather stiffly and at attention, he wasn't his usual, relaxed self. I was confused. We had established a solid friendship, and we were always relaxed when we spent time together. I said hello, and invited him inside. He refused my invitation, which was all the more unlike him. He always came inside.

He took a step backward, and began delivering what seemed to be a memorized speech. "Hello Anila. I am calling on you on behalf of my family. We know that this must be a difficult time for you because you are celebrating the birth of Jesus Christ, and you are in the Muslim world where we do not commemorate this event. We want you to know that we have respect for Jesus Christ. We respect the message of peace and love he taught, but he is not our prophet. Muhammad is our prophet, but this does not mean we do not respect Jesus Christ and his teachings. We also know you exchange gifts at this time of the year, and we wanted to show you our love and respect and give you this gift."

Ashraf, a devout Muslim, then presented me with a package that had been tucked under his right arm. The package was wrapped in a brown paper bag that had been meticulously cut to size, around the brown paper was a thin piece of white string tied into a neat bow.

I accepted the gift with a surprised and gracious, "Thank you," and I invited Ashraf into my apartment, again. He refused my invitation, saying, "No, thank you. I do not want to intrude on you during this meaningful time. I came to deliver the gift, and I will leave now."

I asked him inside two more times. He refused unwaveringly, telling me, "I know this is a special time, and you need time alone." He thought he was doing me a favor, and I couldn't convince him otherwise. He wasn't about to budge. So, I bade him goodbye.

I would have loved the company. I'd been crying that evening because it was Christmastime, and I was feeling very far from home and sorry for myself because I was sitting in the heart of the Arab world. I was missing loved ones and traditional celebrations something fierce. I'm also an extrovert and I love being with people, especially during the holiday season.

I didn't have a clue what was inside the package he'd given to me. I sat on my couch, peeled back the brown-paper wrapping, and gasped. I was stunned.

The gift was painted by Ashraf's brother, Ahmed, a professional artist. Ahmed knew that this painting, out of all of his paintings, meant the most to me. He knew this because I'd spent a luxuriously long afternoon with him in his tiny, brick-and-mortar art studio with a dirt floor and no air conditioning, situated next to the humble family house. I savored his paintings one by one, discussing each painting with him. When I came to this particular painting I sat motionless. Transfixed, I looked at it for at least five minutes without saying anything. When I finally looked up from the painting, my eyes met Ahmed's eyes, and he said to me, "You recognize this place, don't you. You, too, have visited there." "There" was a place I had visited in my deepest and most meaningful meditations. I was in the presence of a talented artist and devout Muslim, and he, too, had been "there" in his meditations, and had painted a visual representation.

This gift came from a place of profound generosity, and deep wisdom. It embodied a clear understanding both of my culture's custom of gift giving at Christmastime, and of the deepest stratum of my soul.

I sat for a long time on that December evening looking at the painting, and whispering prayers of thanks while tears ran down my cheeks. I cried because I was deeply moved that this Muslim family, of modest means, had gifted me with a painting which could have been sold for a meaningful amount of money. Offering it as a gift was more important to them than monetary gain.

I cherish this painting. It is the richest and most meaningful Christmas present I have ever been given. It is a symbol of a place of love and respect that is big enough to hold every one of us when we are open enough to inhabit it.

Chapter 58

SAINT ANDREW'S BALL AND THE MARLBORO MAN

Last night I whooped it up at the annual and gala Saint Andrew's Ball, a black-tie affair, presented by the Khartoum Caledonian Society at the lavish residence of the British ambassador. In the large entryway I was greeted by a band of off-key Sudanese bagpipers who were dressed in kilts, and who didn't know one thing about playing the bagpipes other than to blow mightily. The sound emanating from those bagpipes was dreadful, but it was so awful it was funny, and it made me and everyone else laugh, too. For that reason it helped to set the stage for a fun party.

Thirty minutes later I was standing at a podium in front of two-hundred guests who were seated at tables, set for eight, on the beautifully-groomed lawn. Five men gave speeches and toasts, and then I gave the final toast in Scottish Gaelic with an English translation. When the master of ceremonies introduced me, he told the audience, "... she is about to give a toast that has been sent to Khartoum by the Seattle Gaelic Society in Seattle, Washington in the United States of America." Thank heavens for the Seattle Gaels who sent the toast to me in time for my presentation.

Dinner was fabulous. The freshly smoked Scottish salmon was a real treat. Bottles of Scotch whiskey graced every table, and an unending supply of wine and beer were available at the outdoor bar, truly a luxury in a dry country. Loads of food had been catered by the Khartoum Hilton. (I presumed the haggis was flown in for the occasion.)

The menu was printed on the evening's official program:

Bill O' Fare
Smoked Scottish Salmon
Vegetable Consommé
Deluxe Buffet
Haggis
Dessert
Cheese and Biscuits
Tea/Coffee

After dinner we danced traditional dances on the lawn including Dashing White Sergeant, Cumberland Reel, Eightsome Reel, Gay Gordon, Strip the Willow, and Hamilton House. In preparation, I'd gone to dance practice every Wednesday at the local Sudan Club (run by the Brits for nearly one hundred years). Our teacher, Charlene, had to work mighty hard to get her clumsy troops in order for the big night of dancing. To keep us in line she told us a story about, "… a chap who had too much to drink last year and traveled around the dance floor like an unguided missile, and while he was attempting to dance he kicked the ambassador's wife in the shins and made her fall to her knees!"

I had a blast dancing at top speed in my above-the-knee, chic, dusty-rose, cocktail dress. The only trouble was that a Sudanese man fell madly in love with me, and began following me around while professing his love in broken and drunken English, "Ooh lah lah. You are so beauty. I watch you all night. You are most beauty I ever seen. Marry me. I am good Muslim. I am already marry, but I can have four wife. I want only my wife, and you." He'd had way too much to drink, and kept trying to dance with me, and smooch me. I ended up grabbing a big sweet young Swiss man named Kristof who I knew had a crush on me. I asked Kristof's permission to inform the Sudanese suitor that, "Kristof is my one true love." Kristof heartily agreed. It worked like a charm, and the Sudanese guy disappeared.

The Sudanese fellow wasn't the only one who'd had too much to drink. Toward the end of the evening an Irishman, dressed in traditional regalia including a proper kilt, stood up and yelled, "Speech! Speech! Speech!" After gaining everyone's attention, he trashed the British ambassador and all the citizens of England for repressing the Irish and Scots for centuries. Several embarrassed guests tried to quiet the man, but he wouldn't have any of it. He succeeded in delivering a scathing, slurred speech for a full fifteen minutes.

The clock struck 2 a.m. and I was still going strong, but Elizabeth and her date, with whom I'd arrived, told me they were leaving the party. Kristof offered to drive me home. He and I left the party an hour later, but not before he grabbed and dragged a twenty-foot-long piece of purple velvet off one of the buffet tables. He wrapped the entire piece of fabric around a Scottish man who was tipsy, and had been wandering the grounds unsteadily while whining, "I can't find my dinner jacket, and I'm chilly!" He looked like a discarnate mummy as he stumbled around the groomed lawn, mumbling, while encased in purple velvet in the nippy, 75 degree, midwinter, evening air.

At that point I thought to myself, Considering the sloshed Sudanese man who proposed marriage to me, the drunken Irishman's tirade, the wandering mummy, and many other people who are in various stages of inebriation, it's no wonder some countries outlaw alcohol. And, what would Saint Andrew, the first of the twelve apostles and the patron saint of Scotland, think about these shenanigans? Hopefully, a sense of humor and forgiveness are in his repertoire of saintly characteristics.

I was a little bit nervous about leaving the ambassador's residence at 3 a.m. with Kristof because, although we were far from intoxicated, we'd both been drinking alcohol. Alcoholic consumption is against the law in Sudan, and there is a nightly curfew in Khartoum which is strictly enforced. Roadblocks are set up at midnight, and manned by rifle-toting soldiers. I was apprehensive about how Kristof would respond to the soldiers at the roadblocks, and about how the soldiers would respond to us in return. I didn't want any trouble.

The ride home turned out to be yet another circumstance of, Mafee mushkala, or, The problem is not available. Because, once the soldiers peered inside Kristof's car, they pointed their rifles to the ground and greeted us with big smiles along with a chorus of, "Kreestof! Kreestof!" which they said almost as if in adoration. In return Kristof greeted them with the standard Sudanese greeting, "Al salaam aleikum!" and we drove merrily on our way.

I was simultaneously dumfounded and exhilarated as we departed from the first roadblock. I asked Kristof what in heaven's name was going on. He explained to me, "I made the rounds around town my first week in Khartoum and I gave all the curfew soldiers, at all the roadblocks, packages of Marlboro cigarettes which I brought with me when I came to Khartoum."

Thanks to the illusory Marlboro man, we made it home with ease that night through all of the roadblocks. The brilliant advertising campaign of the rugged Wild West cowboy paved our way through curfew barricades in camel country, in the Sahara desert, where horses and cowboys don't exist, but where real men with their cigarettes thrive.

Chapter 59

SAVING MY SKIN

What do you think you would wear on desert excursions when temperatures top 130 degrees?

Here's a description of the outfit I've devised.

On my legs I wear ankle-length, light-brown tencel pants. I've discovered that tencel breaths well, and it keeps its shape in these harsh climatic conditions. On my upper body I wear a light-blue, long-sleeve, cotton work shirt, buttoned to the top. Around my head I wrap, and then twist together, two oversize cotton scarves and I pull them down to my eyes. On my eyes I wear a large pair of sunglasses. On my feet I wear ankle-length hiking socks and hiking boots. For the finishing touches, I smear lip balm on my lips, and I put the container in my breast pocket along with a container of sun screen so I can re-lather myself after I sweat off the original coating. Also, I slather my entire body with a strong layer of sunblock before I put on the aforementioned clothes. For the finishing touch, I sling a three-quart plastic container of boiled water over my shoulder and across my chest. My body is thus protected from the sun, my feet are protected from the burning-hot sand and the scorpions, and I have enough water to stay hydrated for the day.

Thank God for the invention of sunblock. Without it, my super-white Scottish-French skin would burn to a crisp in less than a half-hour. Dark skin is a godsend for surviving this intense sun. Regardless of the color of one's skin, in this climate the smart thing to do is to stay covered. It's understandable for men to wear turbans and long, loose, flowing gowns or robes and for women to wear headscarves, veils and flowing outfits of ankle-length fabric. I see these garments as a necessary adaptation to, and protection from, the unyielding desert sun and constant wind. The tradition of wearing this type of clothing makes sense when you live here.

Chapter 60

SHOOTING ON
THE STREETS

Shooting rifles into the air is a quirky tradition in some Sudanese celebrations. If I'm outside on my deck and I hear shooting, I always run inside. I figure that what goes up must come down, and the bullets they're shooting into the air have to be landing somewhere in the neighborhood. I want to make sure they don't land on, or in, me.

The first time this happened I thought the revolution had come, and I ran from my deck inside my apartment with my heart pounding. I was trembling and scared to death.

My neighborhood was puzzlingly quiet and peaceful. So, after about ten minutes, I crept outside onto my deck, and peered around the neighborhood. Since I didn't see any military presence I decided the coast was clear, but I was stumped regarding what had actually taken place.

Weeks later, when I asked a Sudanese friend about the ruckus I heard that day, she told me, "Rifles are often shot during celebrations. The shooting of the rifles that day in your neighborhood had probably announced the engagement of a man and woman who live in your neighborhood."

Now I know, but it would have eased my heart palpitations if someone had informed me of this Sudanese tradition before I encountered it in the first place.

Chapter 61

SUDANESE DENTISTRY

Imagine experiencing the worst toothache of your life in one of the poorest countries on the African continent, and you know it would be difficult to take time off from your demanding job because there is no one qualified to fill your shoes. Would you leave that country and have the dental work done in a different country where you trust the dentists and their methods? Or, would you stay and have the work done in that country? What would you do?

I'll tell you what I did.

My tooth started aching the last two hours of work on a Thursday. I've suffered through several root canals, and I recognized the pain. It's one of a kind, and intense. I knew I needed a root canal procedure done immediately. Thursday in Sudan is our Friday in the States; it was the end of the work week for me. By the time I got home I was in agonizing pain. My buddy, Kristof, happened to stop by my apartment to say, "Hi, do you want to do something tonight?" After he saw how much I was hurting, he invited me to go to his apartment and look in the first aid kit his mother, who is a registered nurse, had sent to him. I accepted Kristof's invitation.

At Kristof's apartment, desperation led me to do something I can hardly believe I did. With Kristof translating his mother's German notes into English, I took a pill that Kristof told me was marked, by his mother, as the strongest painkiller in the kit. I did not have the slightest idea what that pill was, and I swallowed it. Within minutes I could hardly keep my eyes open, or carry on a conversation. Kristof drove me home after handing me enough of those pills to last for a week. After being totally zonked-out for the following four days, the pain was getting worse. I knew I had to leave the country, or find a dentist in Khartoum.

I spent the next two days talking to everyone I encountered, asking each person the same question, "Is there a dentist in Khartoum you would recommend?"

To a person, they recommended the same two dentists with the same two cautions, saying the following to me, "There are two dentists in Khartoum who do decent dental work. They were each trained in Europe. All the other dentists are terrible, and you'll leave their offices in worse condition than before you went in. Of the two who are decent, one always produces quality dental work, but no one is sure if he sterilizes his equipment properly. The other dentist always sterilizes his equipment, but the quality of his work varies. Sometimes he's excellent and other times, well, he's not so good."

I ask you, Which dentist would you choose?

I chose the one who sterilizes his equipment, and I hoped and prayed that the quality of his work on me would be excellent.

When I called the dentist's office--and, by the way, I had to make the call from our school's administrative assistant's house since I don't have a phone, and neither do any of my friends--I was told, "The dentist is booked for the next fourteen months." He was booked for over a year. I couldn't wait one week to see the dentist! I pleaded, and pleaded. They relented and squeezed me into his schedule for the needed root canal. However, they booked me for eight separate appointments of twenty minutes apiece. This sounded haywire to me, and I wondered if I'd have a gaping, painful hole in my mouth between appointments. But what was I to do? I agreed to their terms.

The dentist's office was quite far from my apartment. I couldn't imagine trying to bargain for a taxi ride home, on the dusty streets of Khartoum, in the blistering sun, with an unknown taxi driver after I'd had a partial root canal, eight times over. So, I negotiated a ride to the dentist's office, and back home again, with Mr. Yaqub. He is the taxi driver whom I've hired to drive me home from school every day. I paid Mr. Yaqub an astronomical amount of money, for this part of the world, which amounted to the equivalent of $50.00 in U.S. currency for the eight trips. Mr. Yaqub attempted to hide his emotions behind a poker face, but he was noticeably ecstatic. I was equally pleased with the deal I'd cut.

I went to that dentist with my knees shaking. Within minutes of my arrival, he was petting the top of my head as if I were his favorite cocker spaniel, and I relaxed. Once the crown was seated, he held up a mirror to my smiling face and announced to me, "Now you are more beautiful than ever!"

I told him, "Thank you, and I want you to know that you are the gentlest dentist I have ever encountered, and I have encountered hundreds of hours of dental work in my life. For the first time ever, I had no pain during, or after, any of the eight procedures. What did you do that was so different from dentists in the United States?"

He said, "I do not rush, that is why you have no pain during the work, and no pain the next day. I take the time necessary to be gentle. The dentist does not have to hurt you if he is taking the time to be gentle."

I've recommended him to several people who have asked me about my experience in his dental chair. The results have been mixed. I heard that he really hammered on one guy who most of the Sudanese suspect is a CIA agent, but the motivation on that one isn't too hard to figure out.

When I looked at the bill I was shocked. The total cost for my root canal was 125,000 Sudanese dinars which is the equivalent of just about $75.00 in U.S. currency, but the biggest surprise of all was learning that gentle dentistry is possible. I have weathered many painful root canals, as well as scores of painful fillings. I had no idea that dental work could be pain-free. United States dentists kindly take heed.

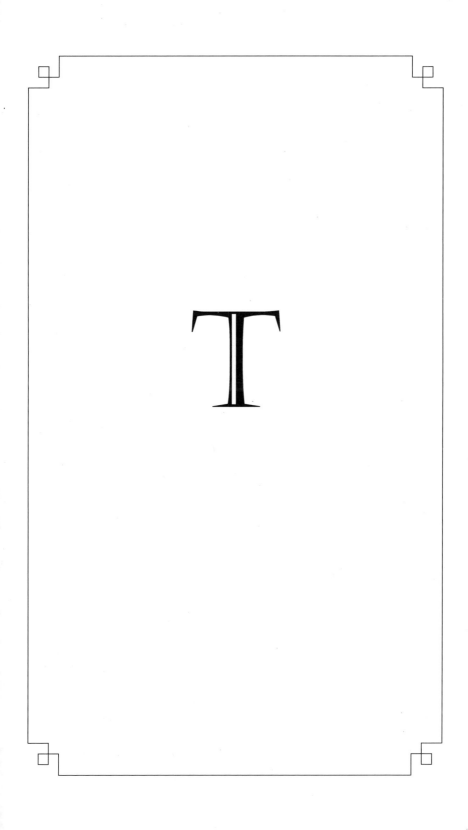

Chapter 62

THE PROBLEM IS NOT AVAILABLE, PEACE

Words are powerful. With our words we create perceptions and thus our reality.

The Sudanese use some of their words and expressions with different approaches to life than we do, and I like the results.

Mafee mushkala is one of my favorite Sudanese expressions. This is said in situations when we, in the United States, say, "No problem." But, here they say, "Mafee mushkala," which means, The problem is not available. Using this sentiment it's easy to get on with living your life productively, and not get bogged down in problems manufactured by your mind. Another way to look at this could be: don't believe everything you are thinking. Furthermore, don't believe what someone else is falsely thinking, and is trying to convince you to believe is true. I think this is an expression that can't be translated exactly, but I like the end result of the translation that was given to me because shifts in perception open the mind, and opening the mind leads to creative thinking followed by the possibility of creative action.

Another excellent word is malesh. A Sudanese friend explained this word to me in the following way, "For example, if you step on someone else's foot by mistake then you say, 'Malesh,' and that means both I'm sorry and it's over now. If the problem is big, or small, the solution is the same.

The way you react to the problem isn't designed by the problem. It's your reaction, it's the way you react to the negative thing that is important."

Malesh is always said with a matter-of-fact tone of voice that has no regret, blame, gossip, or innuendo in it. They say it when it's time to move on, so the present moment can be enjoyed. There is an implicit understanding that regret has the capacity to run one's life, and thus distance one from being in the present because we are preoccupied with regretting what could have, should have, or might have been. Sudanese friends say it to me when something from the past is obviously weighing me down, and it's time to be done with it so I can be happy living my life in the here and now. They say, "Malesh," in circumstances when we'd say, "Get over it." I like the suggestion inherent in malesh because the onus is put on the circumstance, rather than on the person which implies faulting the person for not getting over it. This can lead to difficulties because one cannot change what one blames oneself for. With the attitude embodied in this word, there is an understanding that there is a time to assume productive responsibility, and there is a time to move on, but there is never a time to take your feelings out on someone else.

Now I have a question to ask you: Can you imagine living in a land where the message of peace is exchanged thousands of times throughout every day and night? Such a place exists in Sudan.

The first words the Sudanese say to each other are of peace. Al salaam aleikum means: Peace be with you, or, Peace be unto you, and they say this expression in the same situations when we would say, "Hi," "Hello," or, "Hey!" In response to this greeting, people say, "Wa aleikum el salaam," and this expression wishes peace to the other person in return. Throughout the day and night I greet everyone--friends, gate guards, neighbors, shopkeepers, fellow shoppers, taxi drivers, neighbors--with, "Al salaam aleikum." My greeting is always returned with, "Wa aleikum el salaam," coupled with a sincere Sudanese smile. Of course, many times people say, "Al salaam aleikum," to me first, and I answer with a smile and, "Wa aleikum el salaam." I enjoy these constant and uplifting exchanges.

Ma alsalaam means: with peace. Here you say, "Ma alsalaam," whenever someone is departing a situation. In other words, you say this whenever we, in the U.S. would say, "Goodbye," "Bye," "So long," or, "See ya." For example, you say it to a shopkeeper when you leave his shop, to a taxi driver before you get out of his taxi, when you are leaving to return home after a five-hour visit with friends, after a brief conversation with a neighbor, and it's the last thing you say before you end a phone call. I find saying, "Ma alsalaam," quite meaningful.

I welcome the opportunity to greet and send a person off with a wish for peace. Living in a land where the message of peace reverberates palpably and sincerely throughout the day and night constantly renews my faith in the possibility of harmony between fellow human beings.

The study of languages brings about a deeper understanding and appreciation of cultures. I have studied and spoken Arabic in Sudan, Swahili in Tanzania, Spanish in Colombia and Seattle, and Scottish Gaelic in Seattle. Learning commonly-used expressions can provide insights to perspectives held in that culture. Speaking a language appropriately and respectfully opens doors to indigenous hearts and homes. Along with opening doors, these common Sudanese expressions are useful and meaningful perception changers.

U

Chapter 63

UNSETTLING UNREST

We had quite a scare, during my second springtime in Khartoum, when we heard the news that Sudanese rebel forces were marching toward the dam at Domazine with the intention of taking it over. If the rebels took control of that dam, they would have been in control of the source of all of the electricity in Khartoum. That, most probably, would have led to the takeover of the government by the rebel forces, and that would have resulted in revolution and ensuing chaos in Khartoum, the capital city. If chaos reigned then I, along with every European-looking person in Khartoum, would have stuck out like a sore thumb.

I wondered, Would the Sudanese be as friendly and generous in times of revolution as they are now? I prayed that I didn't have to discover the answer to that question.

For several weeks the city was abuzz with rumors about this potential takeover. I trusted the information I was getting at the Sudan Club every Friday at brunch. During those few weeks, the Friday brunch crowd at the Sudan Club swelled to about twenty expatriate patrons; under normal circumstances only about eight expats would dribble in for brunch. Much of our information came from a Scottish engineer whose job it was to oversee the renovation of the dam at Domazine. The engineer traveled to the dam about twice a week, and he was very familiar with that geographical area of Sudan. One afternoon he told us, "Two days ago I was informed by my local sources that the rebel forces are within fifteen kilometers of the dam. I trust the locals who gave me this information. I've been working with them for months. The takeover of the dam is a very strong possibility. I've ordered my work team to pull out of the dam area. It's imminently dangerous in that area."

When we heard this, we knew the situation was dire.

The American passport-carrying teachers at my school began to have emergency meetings to plan how we could exit Sudan in a big hurry. The spokesperson for our group was supposedly in touch with embassy personnel. He had apparently been told that helicopters from the U. S. would land on the grounds at our school, and fly us to safety. Nice idea, but I wasn't counting on it. It sounded like a long shot to me, a very long shot.

For reasons known only to the rebels, they called a halt to their march when they were within earshot of the dam; and they disappeared into the vast reaches of the desert.

Living with that threat was nerve-racking. I hope that's the closest I ever come to experiencing a revolution.

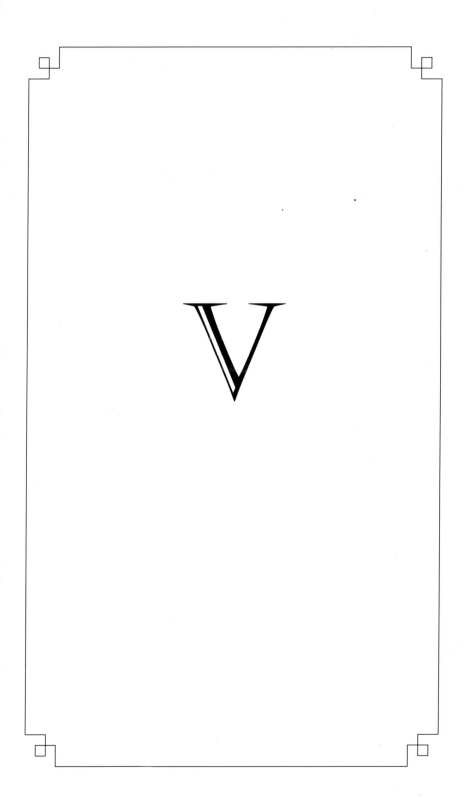

V

Chapter 64

VIGIL FOR THE SICK

Put yourself in my shoes for a minute. Imagine feeling the sickest and weakest you've ever felt in your life, as if you have the worst flu imaginable. You don't have a phone, or email access. You don't know where to find a doctor or a hospital. None of the bus or taxi drivers speak or read English. You live in a neighborhood with indigenous people, and you don't speak the local language. Would you feel frightened? I felt frightened.

This was my situation when I shuffled to answer my front door dressed in a sweat suit over which I'd wrapped two blankets. It was hotter than blazes, but I was freezing. Ashraf was knocking on my door, and ready to give me my weekly Arabic lesson. I told him, "I'm sorry you drove all the way over here today. I can't have my lesson with you. I have a high fever, and I'm too sick to concentrate." I asked him to return the following week.

Ashraf insisted that he drive me, immediately, to a nearby clinic because the symptoms I described to him were those of a type of malaria that causes brain damage within forty-eight hours. I had already been sick for over twenty-four hours. There was no time to lose. I accepted his offer.

Even though the blood tests at the clinic proved negative, Ashraf was firm about staying with me that evening, telling me, "You are too sick to be alone. It is dangerous to be alone when you are this sick." He was right.

He left around 11 p.m. that evening, and promised he'd return early in the morning to check on me. For the following five days Ashraf, several of his cousins, and his sister took shifts staying with me for fifteen hours a day. They arrived each morning at about eight, and stayed until eleven each evening. I don't know how I could have made it through that illness without them. I was too sick to do much of anything for myself. I was so weak I couldn't walk more than about six feet at any one time. My Sudanese friends asked me what I wanted to eat and drink, bought and cooked those foods and beverages, carried them to me as I lay on my living room couch, and made sure I ate and drank them.

Several weeks later, when I was at Ashraf's house, I gave his father a hearty "Thank you!" and I told him how much it meant to me that his extended family members had taken care of me when I was so sick. His gentle, straight-forward response to me was, "You are one of our family, and this is the same thing we would do for our family." I felt thankful that they extended their concept of family to include me. They nursed me back to health by keeping a constant and compassionate vigil over me. They lived according to the Koran, and they walked their talk.

During the following school year I, once again, was very sick with the flu for a week. I had become friends with a teacher from my school who dropped by my apartment every day with food for me to eat, movies for me to watch, and to see if I was feeling better. Several times I had attended services with her, and her husband and kids, at the one and only church in Khartoum. She was a Christian, and she walked her talk.

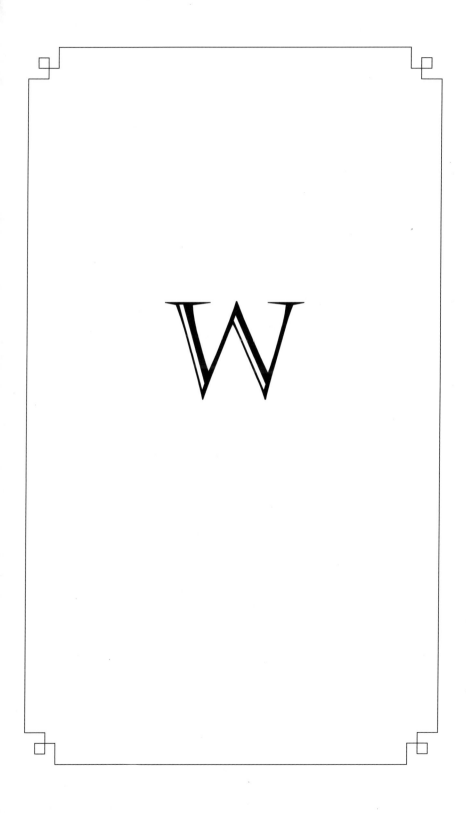

Chapter 65

WAR LESSONS

Every person, every community, and every country has a dark side. The glaring dark side of Sudan has manifested in a civil war that rages in the south of Sudan, destroying lives and demolishing landscapes.

I spoke with many Sudanese people who were unequivocally against the war in the south and, if the rumors were true that genocide was occurring in the west, they were against that, too. They talked openly about being heartsick about the war, but they had no idea what to do about stopping the conflict, and it weighed on them.

Any young, strong male was fair game. I heard several first-hand reports of men between the ages of fourteen and twenty-five who were walking along a street in Khartoum minding their own business when they were grabbed by soldiers, thrown into a military vehicle, and carted off to a holding pen. There they were held, under armed guard, along with hundreds of other young men who would be sent to fight in the war.

A nineteen-year-old Sudanese friend of mine was hauled to a police station and interrogated for seven hours. He managed to convince his interrogators of his student status, and he was set free. If he wasn't a student, he would have been inducted into the army then and there. He related this story to me in a shaking voice, and concluded his tale by telling me, "The ordeal made me feel like I'm not a citizen in my own country."

Since all students were exempt from the army, our school began issuing student identification cards. Prior to initiating this practice, several of our students were snatched by the military police. One was rescued by family members who, when he didn't come home one evening, began a frantic search. The family arrived at the holding pen in their new Mercedes, and his parents paid a high ransom to retrieve their son. But the majority of Sudanese families did not have the cash to reclaim their sons.

When the seizing of young men began happening more frequently, the Sudanese surmised that replacements were needed for the copious amounts of young men who, it seemed, had been killed in the fighting.

A direct result of any war is refugees, and one day our upper-school students traveled on a chartered bus to visit a school for children who were refugees from the war in southern Sudan. We arrived bearing the gifts of drinks, cookies, and zeers--clay containers for holding and keeping water cool--for the students and the staff in their school at East Gerief.

The students from our school were from upper-middle and upper-income families from all over the world, as well as from Khartoum. The words below represent their observations and resulting life-changing experiences which resulted from our brief and meaningful visit.

One student shared the following:

> When I entered the first classroom I was choked up because in my mind I was wondering how could these students manage to sit on broken benches. They were so close to each other, and I had no idea how they could concentrate on their studies. I was astonished because I had never in my life seen classrooms made out of bamboo sticks. I felt sorry for those students who had to sit every day in the heat for at least six hours in Sudan where the sun is really hot. I felt sad to see such innocent people suffering. On our way back to our school I was thinking about how can I create solutions to solve their problems.

Another student shared this:

> I thought that the water project we were doing was merely a project. It turned out I was wrong. At first my friends and I just wandered around staring disbelievingly

at the school. We were greeted by a sight I'll never forget. There were all these kids, dirty and dressed in tattered rags, yet singing and dancing inside the dark and dusty classrooms. Their voices were loud and rhythmic as they chanted their exotic African songs. I wondered how kids as frail looking as them could have all that energy. Their happiness was contagious and soon I found myself singing and shouting with them. I felt as if I was sharing something with them, as if they were old friends. Later I went to look at the water pots we had built for them. They looked great. I was glad I was helping to make a difference, no matter how little. Compared to these kids all my complaints were nothing. I could learn a thing or two from them.

And a third student shared:

I wouldn't say that I ever saw anything like that before. I didn't understand how anybody could be so happy with so little. Walking to school barefoot turned their soles as hard as leather, but still every one of them had a very pleased look on their face. When I turned around to see who was following me, I saw a little boy with a shy face looking at me. I slowly went to him and shook his hand. Never in my life did I feel such hard palms for a child of his age. I tried to compare my childhood with that little boy who is missing all the fun of his childhood and will never have a second chance to get it back. I don't know if I could forget him, and something in me changed forever. I had never learned so much about the real world in one day as I learned from that trip.

I was inspired by the understanding and empathy that was ignited inside my students. This led me to think that if the wealthier children of the world were given the opportunity to experience the circumstances of children who are the victims of war, as well as those who live with very few material advantages, our world could potentially become a more equal place for all. True understanding and empathy guide the path to meaningful action.

Chapter 66

WHIRLING DERVISHES

"Stark-raving mad!" were the words used by several Sudanese women to describe the whirling dervishes to me.

In my opinion, these Sufi mystics are madly in love with God.

I experienced these madly whirling dervishes three times. I would have gone more often had their mosque been closer to where I lived. To reach the mosque, Sudanese friends drove me for an hour along dusty, dirt thoroughfares, and through a maze of back roads on the outskirts of Khartoum. I am thankful to my friends because I could never have found that mosque on my own.

The dervishes whirled in front of their mosque, named Hamed al Nil, every Friday in the late afternoon. They were the most energized and spiritual human beings I've ever witnessed. It's difficult to give an apt description on paper because the energy of these beings needs to be experienced first hand, but I'll do my best.

The designated whirlers twirled barefoot in the desert sand, on the inside of a large circle. Comprising half of the circle were onlookers, almost all of whom were Sudanese, and this was where I stood. The other half of the circle was comprised of approximately two-hundred Sudanese men, all of whom were dressed in pure-white jalabeyas. They were packed shoulder to shoulder in a tight semicircle. They chanted, "God is one," in Arabic, and swayed back and forth in time to the beating of large, upright drums and to the ringing of tambourines which were played by dark-skinned men who were wearing their hair in a style similar to dreadlocks.

My favorite Sufi whirler wore a dress made of a patchwork of multicolored rags with gold bells and trinkets sewn onto the fabric. He held a stick with copper wire wrapped around it. His body twitched as he danced and shuffled. Both he and his stick looked as if, at any moment, he or it could jump up and fly around in the air, anointing people with blessings and healings. My other favorite whirler wore a thick, dreadlock-style hairdo. He was wearing a bright-green, ankle-length dress which was draped with enormously long necklaces made of hundreds of small, round, wooden prayer beads. There was an aged, toothless man in a bright-green dress who walked around carrying a big pot of smoking incense. He stopped in front of me and shouted, "Come on! Come on!" So I encircled myself, using my hands to surround my body, with his billowing, gray, incense smoke. He then moved on to other onlookers, and invited them to "Come on!" and some did so.

As the afternoon progressed, many of the men when the spirit moved them, broke rank and danced away from the semicircle and into the center area, where they turned over and over in ecstatic, consecutive summersaults in the sand. At sundown the outside ceremony concluded, and the men went inside the mosque to continue their worship. Elated children held a single, long, slender, white piece of fabric, and laughed as they ran through the adjoining graveyard that sprawled across the flat, rocky, rust-brown desert.

The dervishes are true mystics who are ecstatically in love with God. Their love and devotion is palpable. I could feel it permeate my body, mind, and spirit during each of the three times I had the honor of being in their presence.

I was familiar with the chants intoned by these Sufi men because I had chanted the same chants several years ago when I spent an inspiring week at Northwest Sufi Camp near Seattle on Vashon Island. Being in the midst of this ceremony in Sudan brought back memories of that week when I experienced a state of spiritual unity as I, along with about a hundred others, intoned the chants while we moved together in a large circle. I had not heard these chants since that summer experience on Vashon. As I watched and listened to the Sudanese Sufis I felt myself falling into an effortless, ecstatic state of oneness with God once again.

Chapter 67

WOMEN'S CLOTHING AND CULTURAL CHAMELEONS

Surprise! Muslim Sudanese women do not wear black, do not wear veils, and their faces are clearly visible at all times. In actuality, a few women do wear black veils. My best guess is that about one in every 250,000 women wears them in Khartoum. That leaves about 249,999 women out of every 250,000 with their faces showing. Thus another stereotype flies out the window.

Many women bedeck their bodies in a traditional tobe made of screamingly bright fabric. The tobe is more or less the Sudanese equivalent of an Indian sari. Each tobe is made of one piece of fabric that is five yards long. The cloth is wound around the entire body, from ankle to head, with the top-most piece draped around the head and hair. A woman can really express herself with the fabric she chooses to wear and, believe me, there is no shortage of colorful tobe fabrics. I swear that I've seen some of the most vivid textiles on the face of the planet on the streets of Khartoum.

The tobe is almost always wound around a voluptuous body. Sudanese women, young and old alike, do like to eat and as a result they are hefty. Hefty is considered beautiful, and I'm told that their men like them that way. Thick ankles are desirable, too. Calorie counting causes no stress because it does not exist here.

Most of the older women dress in tobes. Most of the younger women dress in ankle-length, A-line skirts, and on top they wear a loose-fitting blouse or T-shirt. They always cover their heads, as required by law. They usually wear a gauzy, see-through scarf made of a light-weight mesh fabric in a variety of pretty colors ranging from bright to pastel. I've been told that, in accordance with Sudanese law, Sudanese women have to keep their heads covered at all times when in the company of men; if they don't abide by this law, they can be put in jail.

One of the ways I show my respect for this culture is by wearing clothes that show as little skin as possible. I dress in blouses and cotton tops that are loose fitting with sleeves that come down to my elbows, and necklines that are close to my neck. Along with that, I usually wear an A-line skirt that is mid-calf length. I do not cover my head because this is not my tradition, and it is not required of me according to Sudanese law. When I first arrived, I tried to keep a scarf on my head to show respect. However, I found that this is an art I could not master in the constant desert wind which continually stole my scarf off my head; it was such a bother I gave up trying. Fortunately no one looks askance at me. I am excused from the headscarf law because I am a foreigner.

Speaking of mandatory headscarves, I have a poignant story to tell. In the privacy of her home, a beautiful, devout, Muslim woman in her mid-twenties told me, "I am a devout Muslim, but I do not believe the Koran requires women to cover their heads. I will not perform music wearing a headscarf. If I go on stage without covering my head, they will stop the performance and take me to jail. I have chosen to give up my career for what I believe." My Sudanese friends told me she had great talent and a promising singing career. To say that I respect this young woman is an understatement. Hearing this story made me appreciate all the more that I can, for the most part, wear what I want to wear in the United States.

I heard another account of a woman who was picked up by the Khartoum police, and taken to jail because of the way she was dressed. She'd left home to go shopping in an open-air market dressed in skin-tight blue jeans, stiletto heels, a skin-tight and low-cut top with heaps of gold jewelry nestled in her exposed cleavage. She hailed from the Horn of

Africa, and her U.S. husband had to go to the jail to retrieve her. It's not a surprise that the police picked her up. This was a flagrant violation of Sudanese standards of decency.

Rules and standards of good taste vary from culture to culture; conformity to those societal norms is expected and required in every culture. If one wants to travel or live in another country successfully, one must be willing to bend to the prevailing customs and laws in the host country.

One sure strategy for staying out of trouble, and for opening foreign doors, is to dress according to local custom. I have named this the art of being a cultural chameleon. This doesn't necessitate giving up who you are at your core. It simply means temporarily changing your superficial colors, or changing clothes in this case, so you fit in and are accepted. Being a cultural chameleon makes for a more meaningful, enjoyable and trouble-free experience.

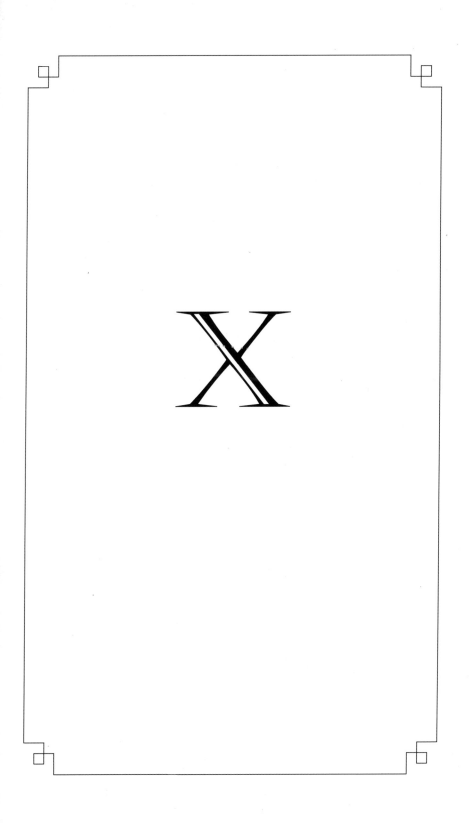

Chapter 68

XENOPHOBIA AND THIN BLOOD

Over and over again, in broken English, I was told by Sudanese Muslims, "I have something tell you. You change my opinion Americans forever." In other words, I was told by countless Sudanese that I had changed their opinion about Americans for the good, forever. Since the Sudanese are aptly described as being "disarmingly honest," I took these words as an honest compliment. Each Sudanese person who said this to me would approach me with the same, intense sincerity, and they stood with their face close to mine and looked directly into my eyes while talking to me. None of the Sudanese who said this to me knew each other.

The first few times someone expressed this sentiment, I was stunned. Before long, I knew what to say in return. I assured them, "I have many friends who are just like me, and there are many, many Americans just like me." Each time I had this interchange I felt a renewed spark of hope that a greater peace in our world is possible, and it can be fostered and sustained by one interaction at a time.

The Sudanese also frequently told me that I had "demeek khafeef" which literally means to have thin blood. In actuality it refers to someone who laughs and smiles easily, and is an easy person to be around and to get along with. I'd also been told many times that I had "a face full of light."

I greatly appreciated their acceptance of me despite their opinion about Americans in general.

When I asked Sudanese people to tell me their impression of Americans, they answered with a variation on the same theme, and would say, "Our impression of Americans is that they party too much, drink too much alcohol, laugh loudly and artificially, live hollow and superficial lives, talk out of both sides of their mouth and are not sincere." These sentiments were based on the unbecoming behavior of a small contingent of visible Americans who had lived and worked in Sudan.

The negative notions the Sudanese have of Americans also stem from the fact that they have been influenced by their press against Americans, just as we Americans have been influenced by our press against Muslims. Sudanese meet few Americans, just like we have met few Sudanese and few Muslims. Unfortunately, this has lead to xenophobia in both cultures. It's time to take an honest look at what hating and being fearful of what is foreign and different has brought us because, as the Chinese sage Lao Tzu warned us, "If you do not change direction, you may end up where you are heading."

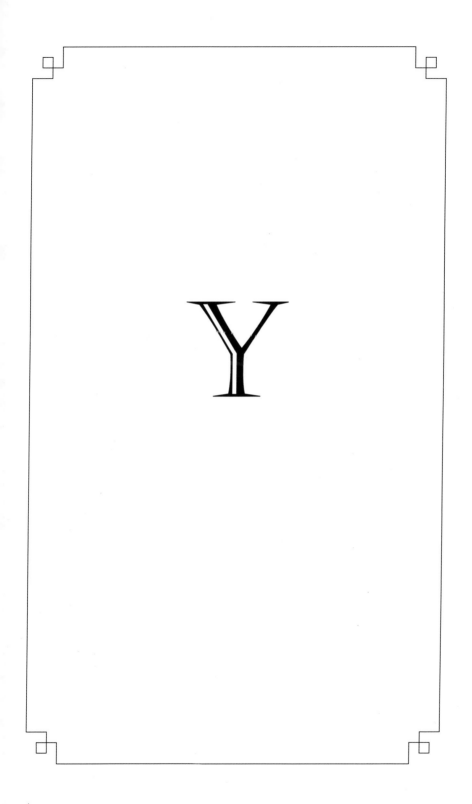

Chapter 69

YORUBA TRIBE DRUMS UP GRANDPA JACK

One of the side benefits of my teaching job in Khartoum was attending, all expenses paid, the annual East African Teachers' Conferences. During my first year of teaching it was held in Nairobi, Kenya, and there I encountered my Scottish ancestors.

How did that happen? Here's the story.

I'd signed up for a Creative Writing for Teachers workshop, and I attended that class my first morning of the conference. For the final writing exercise, the instructor told us to "… focus on the topic of setting and let your writing flow for ten minutes," and he began playing a CD of traditional African drumming.

My first sentence was about Africa, but then I began writing about the Seattle Folklife Festival held at Seattle Center the previous May where I, along with friends and members of my choir, performed and sang traditional songs in Scottish Gaelic. I went on to write about my Scottish grandfather, and when I visited the house in Scotland where he was born. I wrote about my Scottish ancestors and Scotland. There I was in Nairobi, and I could literally feel my Scottish ancestors surrounding me.

The rational sector of my brain began to squawk inside my head, and silently screech, Why am I doing this? This is crazy! The designated topic is setting. I'm sitting in Africa. The background music is African drumming.

I'm supposed to be writing about Africa! Why am I compelled to write about everything Scottish?

The intuitive side of my mind prevailed. I continued writing about Scotland.

When the ten minutes concluded, our instructor invited the class participants to read what they had written. Each person, one by one, read what he or she had written on the designated topic of setting. Everyone with the exception of me. I passed. I was too embarrassed to read. Everybody in the class had written about, you guessed it, about Africa. How could I possibly read mine about Scotland? I couldn't bring myself to do it.

After the classroom emptied out, I approached the instructor. I stammered, "I, I was too embarrassed to read my piece of writing because I didn't write about Africa. I wrote about Scotland. I wrote about how much I love to sing traditional songs in Scottish Gaelic." I paused, breathed deeply, and continued, "Scotland! That's where my maternal grandfather came from. I wrote about him. I wrote about when I visited the big, stone house where my grandpa was born in Outerson, Scotland. I felt really close to my Scottish ancestors the whole time I was writing and, and that's what, and who I wrote about. But I, I don't know why I wrote about all of that. That wasn't the topic you asked us to write about. The topic was 'setting.' And we're in Africa." I stopped talking because I felt too puzzled to continue.

The instructor leaned close to me, and said, "The drumming I played during those ten minutes of writing was created and made by the people from the Yoruba tribe in Africa to invoke the spirits of the ancestors. Your Scottish ancestors were invoked by the drumming on the CD. You were the only one in the class who got the real meaning. The real topic wasn't Africa. The real topic was ancestors. Congratulations."

If this story hadn't happened to me, I think I would have a difficult time believing it. Since it did happen, I now trust that we are connected along unseen byways, tributaries, and channels that challenge our immediate comprehension and imagination. We can be more connected than we think, if we let it happen.

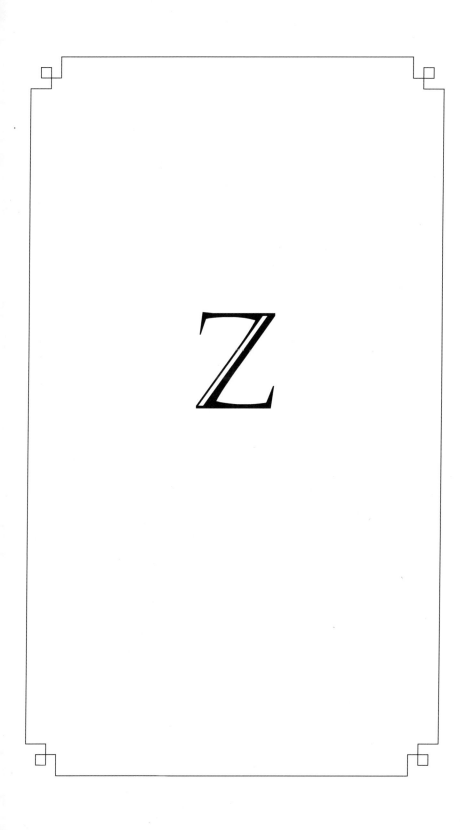

Z

Chapter 70

ZEBRAS AND SCARY MONSTERS

The Sudanese don't celebrate Halloween, but since I teach in an American school we celebrated Halloween with parties in our classrooms and a costume parade. Sudanese and Ethiopian custodians were asked to judge the kids' costumes and, to say the least, something was lost in translation.

The Best Cartoon Character was awarded to a second grader. When the award was announced she remained true to her character as she snarled and hissed, "I'm not a cartoon character. I'm not! I'm a witch. Can't you see?!" and the little witch glared at the judges with utter contempt.

The Most Original was awarded to a first-grade girl prancing around in a prepackaged getup purchased from a mail-order catalogue. Her ensemble consisted of a miniskirt and a halter-top made of green-and-blue iridescent polyester material. To top it off, she flaunted a pink, fluffy boa made of polyester feathers wrapped around her little brown neck. Not one stitch was original.

The prize for the Cutest was awarded to a fifth-grader who held a grotesque, plastic, cutoff head which was oozing fake blood in his left hand, and whose white shirt was pulled over his real, intact, but concealed head. He displayed no resemblance to cute.

It's not fair to fault the judges. They'd been given a hasty explanation of their responsibilities. For the judges to truly understand what they were supposed to be evaluating, careful explaining would have been necessary because there simply isn't any overlap in the cultures regarding the concepts inherent in Halloween costumes. I'm certain the custodians would have been mortified if they had learned the real meaning of the words, especially "cutest," because they are gentle and well-meaning souls.

Later that evening I dressed for an invitation-only Halloween party held at the home of a friend. What do you think I was on Halloween? After all, I was living in Africa so what else would I have been but a zebra. Actually, I did entertain the idea of dressing up as a camel, but I couldn't figure out how to look like a camel and I had everything I needed to look the part of a zebra. Before I left Seattle for Khartoum I'd packed greasepaint just in case I had a Halloween party to attend and now I used it to paint my face, neck, and arms with large, bold, alternating, black-and-white stripes. Then, I carefully pulled a short-sleeve, black, nightshirt over my head, with an embroidered zebra on the front of it (which I bought while on holiday in Nairobi, Kenya). Onto my legs I pulled black tights. Looking at my reflection in the mirror, I said out loud, "Wow, Anila, you look stunning!"

Filled with Halloween enthusiasm, I raced down my stairs, and began prancing down the dirt road in front of my apartment. Since no one in Khartoum dresses in costumes for any occasion, or celebrates Halloween, or knows anything about Halloween, you can imagine what happened. Startled pedestrians looked at me with a combination of bewilderment, apprehension, and fear as they stepped to the sides of the street. I calmed my stride to an unassuming walk. Fortunately the party was only a block from my apartment.

When I entered the party, all the Filipino babies and young children recoiled from me, and shrieked in terror. I was the only one wearing a costume. What's more, I was the only non-Filipino in the room, and most of the Filipinos only came up to my elbows. To the kids I looked like a gigantic, menacing monster instead of the benign zebra I'd set out to be.

Simply stated, Halloween does not translate. But, take it from me, a scary monster could, in fact, be a peace-loving human being waiting and wanting to be discovered and acknowledged.

EPILOGUE: GO IN PEACE

While driving east on Mercer Street near downtown Seattle, I heard startling news on my car radio. The United States had just bombed a chemical-weapons factory in Khartoum. I went into shock. My entire body began to shake; my right foot trembled on the accelerator. My heart began beating hard and fast. I clutched the steering wheel. My mind raced with thoughts, Bomb Khartoum? Bomb the sweet people in Khartoum? Is my Sudanese family alive? Did they die? I can't believe it! Bomb Khartoum? Why?!

Sentiments spoken to me by many Sudanese circled in my head, "You have changed our image of Americans, forever. We had no idea there were Americans like you."

What would the Sudanese believe about Americans now? Now that the United States had bombed Khartoum.

My mind bounced from belief to disbelief as I thought, Bomb? No! Khartoum? Is this true? It can't be true! Why?

My gas gauge was on empty. I had to stop and get gas.

"Breathe," I told myself out loud, "Breathe deeply. Watch the road. Concentrate. Watch the traffic. Stop at a gas station. Get gas. Breathe."

I pulled into a gas station, and parked my car beside a gas pump. I didn't want to stay out of my car for any longer than absolutely necessary. I had to get back to the radio and the news. As I dashed into the office, I felt nauseated and my body trembled. I slapped a five-dollar bill on the counter, and said, "I want five dollars of gas."

The attendant handed the bill back to me. I slapped the five dollars into his hand, and he handed the five-dollar bill back to me again.

I tried to control my emotions, but I knew I sounded on edge and demanding as I said, "I want five dollars worth of gas. I'm trying to give you the five dollars to pay for it!"

He matched my tone, and protested, "This is a one-dollar bill. You want five dollars of gas and you handed me one dollar. I need five dollars from you!"

Hands shaking, I dug into my wallet. As I handed him five dollars, I unraveled and began crying. I sputtered through my tears, "I'm sorry. I'm so sorry. I just heard the news on the radio, and the United States bombed Khartoum. I just came back to the United States after two years of teaching in Khartoum and, and Sudanese people are the sweetest people. I have dear friends there and I, and I."

I starting sobbing so hard and I couldn't finish my sentence.

Tears welled up in the eyes of the gas station attendant. His voice softened. He looked at me in disbelief as he said, "Khartoum? Bombed Khartoum? I am an Ethiopian refugee and a Christian. I was a refugee in Khartoum. I lived in Khartoum. I did not have any money, not one cent when I lived in Khartoum. But, I knew I would never go hungry in Sudan because Sudanese are generous, and nice, and they would never let anyone starve, no matter who they were."

He explained to me that every day, in the late afternoon, he would walk various streets in Khartoum. The first group of impoverished Muslim workers he came upon who were eating their daily traditional afternoon meal of fava bean foul, that group would always invite him to eat with them. They would all sit and eat together along the side of a dusty street. This is how he survived.

I extended my hand to him. We held hands for several minutes as we cried together, connected by our lives in Khartoum and the generosity and caring that had been extended to each of us there. Then he, an Ethiopian Christian and a refugee, and I, a second-generation Seattleite and a believer in a Higher Power, we exchanged a heartfelt, "Ma alsalaam," and I returned to my car.

Several days later more disturbing news arrived; it was announced that the United States had made a mistake. The ostensible Khartoum chemical-weapons factory that had been bombed was, in actuality, a legitimate pharmaceutical factory.

When I heard this report, I asked myself, Do I really believe that a greater peace and harmony on our planet is possible? I knew it was time to reread a quote that I always carry with me. It's written on a piece of paper, now wrinkled and discolored, which I bought years ago from a local calligrapher who was selling her wares next to Christ Church in Oxford, England.

Each time I read it, it restores my confidence:

> If there be righteousness in the heart, there will be
> beauty in the character. If there is beauty in the character,
> there will be harmony in the home. If there is harmony in
> the home, there will be order in each nation. When there
> is order in each nation, there will be peace in the world.

The origin of these words is shrouded in mystery. At the bottom of my quotation it states, Very Old Chinese Proverb. I have read that it is attributed to Buddhism, or perhaps to Taoism. Other sources state that Confucius was the first to say it. It is also credited to the East Indian guru Sai Baba. What's more, I have seen it intricately embroidered, framed, and hung on a wall in a Scottish home and titled A Scottish Blessing. From which person and from what culture it originated is not important. The point is to take personal responsibility for living the universal wisdom it contains.

GLOSSARY OF ARABIC WORDS AND NAMES

Abu Medino (pronounced au-boo med-een-oo, accent on boo and een) the father of Medino

afwan (pronounced af-waun, accent on af) you're welcome

Allah (pronounced awh-luh, accent on awh) the name of God in Islam

Allah kareem (pronounced awh-luh car-eem, accent on awh and eem) **Allah** is the name of God in Islam and **kareem** means generous or good; these two words together mean God is generous or God is good

al salaam aleikum (pronounced all sah-laum all-lake-oom, accent on laum and lake) peace be unto you, peace be with you, go in peace

angareb (pronounced on-greeb, accent on greeb) a traditional Sudanese bed made of four hand-hewn wooden posts strung together with rope woven tightly into macramé knots

anna meen Amrica (pronounced an-uh meen um-ree-kuh, accent on an, meen, and ree) I am from America

Arous (pronounced ah-roos, accent on roos) a resort on the Red Sea in Sudan

asswad hamsajamil (pronounced ass-wad ham-suh-juh-meel, accent on ass and ham) five pretty eggplant (note: this was taught to me by my taxi driver and I can't vouch for the accuracy of the translation)

Atbara (pronounced at-bar-uh, accent on at) a city in Sudan

baba ganoush (pronounced bawbaw guh-noosh, accent on the first baw and noosh) a food made from roasted eggplant that is peeled and then mashed with **tahina**, olive oil, and lemon juice

becum (pronounced bay-come, accent on bay) how much

baksheesh (pronounced back-sheesh, accent on sheesh) depending on the situation this means tip, bribe money, or spare change

demeek khafeef (pronounced dem-eek kau-feef, accent on eek and feef) literally means to have thin blood, in actuality means someone who laughs and smiles easily with people

dinar (pronounced din-ar, accent on ar) the currency during the years I was in Sudan; due to inflation the exchange rate of dinars fluctuated during the 364 days I was in Sudan, as is reflected in the text

East Gerief (pronounced east jur-eef, accent on eef) located in the south of Sudan, literally means the east, small, Nile River bank

Eid (pronounced eed) known as the festival of sacrifice and is a religious event observed on the tenth day of the final month of the Islamic lunar calendar

foul (pronounced fool) fava beans that are cooked until tender and mashed with spices

haboob (pronounced huh-boob, accent on boob) fierce windstorm

Hadendoa (pronounced hah-den-doo-aw, accent on den) a nomadic tribe

Hajj (pronounced hawj) pilgrimage to Mecca

halwah (pronounced hall-wuh, accent on hall) crushed sesame seeds mixed with a syrup, usually honey, to make a flaky confection

Hamed al Nil (pronounced hah-maud el neel, accent on hah) the name of the sheik who is buried in a tomb where the present-day dervishes whirl in Khartoum

haram (pronounced har-aum, accent on aum) forbidden sin

inshaa Allah (pronounced in-shaw awh-luh, accent on shaw and awh) God willing

itfadalay (pronounced it-fau-duh-lay, accent on fau) you are welcome here

jalabeya (pronounced jawl-uh-bee-uh, accent on bee) the traditional dress for Sudanese men; a flowing, mid-calf length, A-line, white, cotton garment with a scoop neck or V-neck

jebel (pronounced jeh-bull, accent on jeh) hill or mountain

jer-jer (pronounced jeer-jeer, accent is equally on both syllables) a green vegetable similar in taste and appearance to arugula

jertik (pronounced jair-tick, accent on jair) a pre-wedding ceremony

jinn (pronounced jin) spirit, such as a ghost

karkaday (pronounced car-kuh-day, accent on car) tea made from hibiscus flowers

Kassala (pronounced caw-suh-luh, accent on caw) a city in Sudan

Khartoum (pronounced car-toom, accent on toom) the capital city of Sudan

kida katir (pronounced kee-duh kuh-teer, accent on kee and teer) this is too much

kofta (pronounced cough-tuh, accent on cough) ground beef, bread, and spices rolled into meatballs or sausages and baked

Koran (pronounced core-an, accent on an) Islam's holy book and sacred text

kwaga (pronounced kwah-juh, accent on kwah) a foreigner

la (pronounced law) no

ma alsalaam (pronounced mah all-saw-laum, accent on mah and lam) go in peace

mafee mushkala (pronounced mah-fee moosh-kuh-luh, accent on mah and mooosh) the problem is not available, no problem

malaki alharris (pronounced maw-law-key al-haw-ris, accent on law and haw) guardian angel

malesh (pronounced mah-lesh, accent on lesh) it's over, it's finished, the problem is gone, sorry

marhaba (pronounced mar-hob-uh, accent on hob) welcome

Meroe (pronounced mer-o-way, accent on mer) a site north of Khartoum where there are ancient pyramids

moya (pronounced moy-yah, accent on moy) water

Muhammad (pronounced moo-haum-ed, accent on haum) the prophet of Islam, also an Arabic male name

Muslim (pronounced muh-slim, accent on muh) followers of the prophet Muhammad, in Arabic this translates as: those who submit to God

Omdurman (pronounced aum-dur-mun, accent on aum) the oldest section of Khartoum

portucan nus kilo (pronounced port-uh-con noos, accent on port and noos; kilo is pronounced the same as we say it in English) a half kilo of oranges

Ramadan (pronounced rom-uh-don, accent on rom) the holy month for Muslims during which there is fasting from food and drink from dawn to sunset

shata (pronounced shaw-tah, accent on shaw) hot sauce made from fresh, very hot, small, green peppers

sheik (pronounced shake) translates as elder, is a term of honor that carries the meaning of leader or governor

shukrun (pronounced shook-run, accent on shook) thank you

shukrun jazeelen (pronounced shook-run juh-zee-len, accent on shook and zee) thank you very much

shwerma (pronounced sh-warm-uh, accent on warm) rotisserie grilled meat or poultry

souk (pronounced sook) market

Souk el-Shabi (pronounced sook el-shaw-bee, accent on shaw) a large market in Khartoum

Suakin (pronounced so-aw-kin, accent on aw) the name of a town and an island in Sudan

Sudan (pronounced sue-dan, accent on dan) currently the third largest country on the African continent

Sudanese (pronounced sue-dan-eez, accent on eez) pertaining to the country of Sudan or its people

tahina (pronounced tah-hee-nuh, accent on hee) a paste-like spread made out of ground sesame seeds

tobe (pronounced tob, with a long o sound) the traditional dress for Sudanese women; more or less the Sudanese equivalent of an Indian sari

tumsah (pronounced toom-suh, accent on toom) crocodile

wa aleikum el salaam (pronounced wauh ah-lake-oom el saul-aum, accent on lake and aum) peace be upon you

zeer (pronounced zear) a container that holds and cools water, made of clay